When You
NEED A
MIRACLE

When You
NEED A
MIRACLE

Stories to Give You Faith
and Bring You Hope

Ann Spangler

ZONDERVAN

ZONDERVAN.com/
AUTHORTRACKER
follow your favorite authors

We want to hear from you. Please send your comments about this book to us in care of zreview@zondervan.com. Thank you.

ZONDERVAN

When You Need a Miracle
Copyright © 2009 by Ann Spangler

This title is also available as a Zondervan ebook.
Visit www.zondervan.com/ebooks.

This title is also available in a Zondervan audio edition.
Visit www.zondervan.fm.

Requests for information should be addressed to:
Zondervan, *Grand Rapids, Michigan 49530*

Library of Congress Cataloging-in-Publication Data

Spangler, Ann.
    When you need a miracle: stories to give you faith and bring you hope /
Ann Spangler.
       p.   cm.
    Includes bibliographical references.
    ISBN 978-0-310-27839-9 (hardcover)
    1. Miracles. 2. Angels—Christianity. I. Title.
    BT97.3.S65—2009
    235'.3—dc22   2009018578

Interior design by Michelle Espinoza

Printed in the United States of America

09 10 11 12 13 14 15 • 22 21 20 19 18 17 16 15 14 13 12 11 10 9 8 7 6 5 4 3 2 1

CONTENTS

INTRODUCTION

We live in an era of anxiety and tremendous uncertainty. To watch the nightly news is to be confronted by stories of financial decline and massive job loss. Millions of people have lost their savings, their homes, and their counted-upon futures. If we haven't suffered such losses, we worry about friends and family members who have or about what the future may hold for us.

If anything good can come from such fears, surely it is the urge to reexamine our lives. What assumptions have we made? What values have we cherished? On what foundation have we built, and will it hold up under all the pressure of the present challenges? When life gets difficult, many people reaffirm the faith they embraced long ago, living it more deeply than ever. Others become open to faith for the first time, sensing their need for God.

Whether you are a person of faith or a person still seeking a faith to embrace, it is likely that you are open to miracles. And if you do not need a miracle right now, you probably know someone who does. That's what this book is about—God doing extraordinary things for ordinary people, surprising us by his goodness and by his power to help us no matter what we may face, now or in the future. I hope that these stories will counter the negativity around you, helping you to feel more secure and at peace as you experience the wonder of belonging to a God who is both more mysterious and more loving than most of us dare to admit or believe.

The poet Elizabeth Barrett Browning once famously wrote that "Earth is crammed full of heaven, and every common bush aglow with God. Those who see take off their shoes." In the pages that follow I will explore stories of miraculous experiences, angelic encounters, and even dreams that reveal something of who God is and how he cares for us. Such stories can help to rekindle our sense of wonder and deepen our sense of awe.

This book is drawn from my earlier books: *An Angel a Day* and *A Miracle a Day*, and, to a much lesser extent, *Dreams: True Stories of Remarkable Encounters with God*. Part 1 contains a brief introduction to the subject of angels and then continues with thematic readings related to angelic encounters in Scripture and in people's lives today. Part 2 provides a brief introduction to the topic of miracles and then continues with thematic readings related to miraculous encounters in the Bible and in the lives of contemporary people.

I hope, through these stories and reflections, to refresh your faith in the God who met Moses in the desert and spoke to him from a fiery bush and to nourish your belief that he still speaks today — telling us of his tender love, assuring us of his power, and reminding us of his goodness. Whether you are reading before a cozy fire or taking a break in the midst of a frenzied day, I hope these stories and reflections will increase your confidence in the love the Father has for you.

This book would not have been possible without the many men and women who were willing to tell their stories about how deeply God has touched their lives. To them I am profoundly grateful. In fact, I received so many responses to my request for stories that I simply didn't have room enough to include them all in the pages of this book. In a few cases, the names of those whose stories are told have been disguised to protect their privacy. Special thanks go to a number of people: Charlene Ann Baumbich, Donna Huisjen, Mark Kinzer, Mary Ann Leland, Patti Matthews, Suzanne Morsefield, LaVonne Neff, Elizabeth Newenhuyse, Pat Springle, Paul Thigpen,

John Topliff, Charles Turner, and Hendrika Vande Kemp. I am also grateful to Sandy Vander Zicht, associate publisher and executive editor at Zondervan, who, from the beginning, caught the vision for this book. Thanks, too, to senior editor at large Verlyn Verbrugge, whose careful work on this and other of my books is greatly appreciated.

NOTES TO THE READER

A number of the Scripture passages quoted in the text refer to "the angel of the Lord." Some biblical scholars believe that this phrase, particularly in the earlier books of the Old Testament, refers to God himself. Others believe that it refers to an actual angel, who closely represents God. Many of the early church fathers tended to recognize the preincarnate Christ in these passages. Whatever the case, readers can fruitfully reflect on these passages, knowing that angels reflect the glory of God and are active in our world only to do his bidding.

It should also be noted that every mention of angels within this book is not necessarily a positive one. Both Scripture and Christian teaching assert the existence of good angelic beings and evil angelic beings. Until Christ's kingdom is fully established, we will have to contend with the activity of Satan and his angels here on earth. Fortunately, they are more than counterbalanced by the power of God at work in us and through us.

PART 1

ANGELIC ENCOUNTERS

Why Talk about Angels?

When I was a less-than-cherubic child of four or five, I entertained a variety of unorthodox notions about the universe and my place in it. Knowing nothing of the Bible at that time, my child's mind tried to make sense out of some of the deeper questions of life. Chief among these was the question of where I had come from.

My parents did their best to teach me my prayers, take me to church, and explain that God deserved the credit for making me. Still, I wondered if God hadn't created me somewhere in the clouds (where I thought heaven was) and only later sent me down to join my family on earth. No doubt I had been influenced by paintings I had seen of chubby little angels bouncing from cloud to cloud, their wings firmly glued to shoulders about the size of mine. More than anything, I wanted to believe that I too had once had wings and would someday have them again. Though I did not understand my desires then, I believe now that I longed for the freedom that the angels possessed and for the ability to move at will between heaven and earth. Somehow, I felt too heavy for my years, unfairly chained by gravity to the natural world when what I wanted was to soar into the skies where I imagined God to be. So strong was my desire to be airborne that, like many children who grew up watching Clark Kent transform himself into Superman, I once attempted a disastrous flight down the living room stairs.

Such experiences were to alter my views drastically. But they did not change my desire for a deeper connection with God and with the unseen world he had created. Years later I have come to understand his mercy and his plan of salvation, accomplished through the life and death of Jesus of Nazareth. I have also come to cherish and to believe the Bible, which tells the unfolding story of God's love for us and his plan for the human race.

Page after page of the Scriptures describe the long struggle between God and the men and women he created to know him. It is a story of mercy, miracles, rebellion, treachery, wrath, repentance, nick-of-time rescues, and ultimate salvation. The cast of characters includes not only the Creator himself and the countless men and women he has made but also angels, both good and bad.

Too often, though, we ignore the role that angels play. Many Christians are afraid that talk of angels will distract from the power and majesty of God. And many others have a hard time taking angels all that seriously. But as John Calvin has said, "The angels are the dispensers and administrators of the Divine beneficence toward us; they regard our safety, undertake our defense, direct our ways and exercise a constant solicitude that no evil befall us."

Like it or not, angels are important players in the drama of salvation. Perhaps it's time we paid a little more attention to these powerful and loving allies that God has given us. True, there are dangers. We must not forget that worship belongs only to God, no matter how beautiful or powerful some of his creatures may be (see Revelation 19:10). We must also remember that angels are but one way that God works in the universe. Pascal said, "We create angels, but trouble comes if we create too many." They aren't the whole story, nor even the most important part of the story. They are simply supporting actors, servants of the living God, as we are. Even so, such fears fail to justify our ignorance of the angels. Knowing more about their nature and purpose will help us to perceive more of God's majesty and his loving plan for our lives.

I have delved into the pages of the Bible and listened to the stories of people of faith in the hopes of satisfying my own curiosity about angels and offering comfort and encouragement to anyone who longs for a deeper connection with God. The skepticism and rationalism of our age have not smothered our desire for the spiritual dimension of life. If anything, such attitudes have merely created a pent-up thirst that only God can quench.

I hope that these reflections will increase your thirst and your desire to know God as you become aware of the heavenly allies he has given you. If we let them, angels can be a window to God, offering a glimpse of his power, his goodness, and his loving intentions toward us. It's time to put aside a materialistic view of the universe in favor of a thoroughly biblical one. With this book, I hope to do in writing what a painter by the name of Sir Edward Coley Burne-Jones accomplished in his art: "The more materialistic science becomes, the more angels shall I paint: their wings are my protest in favor of the immortality of the soul."

1

THE GIFT OF ANGELS

Every good and perfect gift is from above,
coming down from the Father of the heavenly lights.

James 1:17

How would you feel if you gave someone a gift that they refused to open? Wouldn't you be disappointed and a bit hurt? I sometimes wonder if that's how God feels about the angels, wonderful gifts he has given to protect, inspire, and lead us safely home to him. Yet we neglect the angels through our indifference, ignorance, and incorrigible skepticism.

The angels are part of God's ingenious provision for us. Because they are so passionately in love with God, the angels are perfectly conformed to his will. Whatever he tells them to do, they do. Whomever he loves, they can't help but love. Because we belong to God, we can claim the wonderful friendship of angels.

What a tremendous encouragement to know that we are surrounded on every side by loving and powerful protectors. Thinking of angels can ease our sorrows, strengthen our faith, and lighten our hearts. G. K. Chesterton once quipped that "the angels can fly because they take themselves lightly." Of course the angels take themselves lightly. They keep things in perspective in a way that we can't. After all, they live in the presence of God, which means that their vision is clear, unclouded by the confusion and doubts we suffer. Neither do they fall prey to the insidious sin of pride, which weighs us down and chains us to our own small vision of the world. As we learn more about angels and their service, we will learn more about God. Our appetite for the spiritual life will increase and our longing for intimacy with our Creator will grow.

The time has come to open the gift and catch a glimpse of these powerful spiritual beings. Spend a few moments each day with the angels and ask God to use them to show you how lovingly and tenderly he cares for you.

LET WONDER
SURROUND YOU

I charge you, in the sight of God and Christ Jesus and the elect angels, to keep these instructions without partiality.

1 Timothy 5:21

Notice how the apostle Paul reminds Timothy that we live our life under the eye of heaven. As a child, I had a keen sense of the supernatural dimension of life. I was fully convinced, because my parents told me I should be, that God was everywhere and that he was sometimes accompanied by angels. This conviction presented particular problems at bath time. I worried that I was not really alone as I splashed happily in the tub or as I undressed for bed at night. I was glad for God's company but embarrassed that he might be around at indelicate times.

These were childish concerns, of course. But there was something healthy about my acceptance of the fact that life did not end at my fingertips. A world existed that I could not touch or smell or see, yet I knew it was real. As I grew older, my child's worldview narrowed to an adult's, and it was some time before I understood again that life was brimming with wonders, both seen and unseen.

Now I have come to realize that the boundary between heaven and earth is porous, not solid, more like gauze than steel. Though our senses fail to perceive it, the natural and supernatural worlds are constantly impinging on each other. What would it be like, I wondered, if we were to live with a constant awareness of the supernatural dimension of life, if we realized that God is always in the room whether or not we sense his presence? Wouldn't it make a difference in the way we speak, in the way we treat each other, in the way we respond to the stress we face and the fear we feel?

I pose the question not to encourage us to "be on our best behavior" or to try to play-act before God. I've tried that and, believe me, it doesn't work. But knowing that God is present, perhaps we could step back for a moment, asking for his perspective on our lives and on the challenges we face.

Who knows? If we take a moment to call on God today, perhaps he will decide to send an angel or two our way. Whether life feels chaotic or calm right now, ask God for the grace to be mindful of his presence and open to his work.

Lord, restore the innocent wisdom of my childhood. Take away the blinders that keep me from seeing beneath the surface of things. Then give me a glimpse of your grace at work behind the scenes.

THE ANGEL
AND THE OATMEAL

Even the sparrow has found a home
and the swallow a nest for herself,
where she may have her young—
a place near your altar,
O Lord Almighty, my King and my God.
Blessed are those who dwell in your house.

Psalm 84:3–4

Jeanne Phelan was only three years old when she and her brother Jimmy began their search for a new home. With troubles enough of their own, her parents had reluctantly placed them in foster care.

One day Jeanne arrived home from kindergarten and found a shiny, new bike waiting for her. She could hardly believe it. "My foster parents met me, smiling and urging me to ride it. I told them I couldn't wait to show Jimmy. Suddenly their smiles froze. Fear crept over me. Jimmy! Where was Jimmy? I ran into the house and up the stairs into his room. My brother with the tousled hair and the teasing blue eyes, my only link to home and family, was gone. My foster parents had placed him in a home for boys. The bike was a gift to smooth things over.

"That evening, the smell of meatloaf drew me to the dining room table. As I began to eat, I couldn't stop wondering what Jimmy was having for dinner. I began to feel dizzy. Nausea pushed its way up my throat and forced me to the bathroom. A vicious cycle of eating and vomiting ensued. Every morning my foster mother would confront me with a sumptuous breakfast of eggs, bacon, toast, orange juice, and oatmeal. How I hated oatmeal! When I couldn't keep it down, she would become enraged.

"Things got so bad that she finally sent me to a Catholic girls' home. The morning she dropped me off, she told me I would never see Jimmy again. The nuns took one look at me and placed me in the infirmary. A few days later a smiling young sister stood by my bed. She told me that many people had been praying for me and that she believed God was healing me. She said it was important that I learn to eat well, and then she helped me get dressed and walked me to the cafeteria. There on a long table was a steaming bowl of oatmeal!

"I picked up my spoon but was once again assaulted by nausea. Then, suddenly I realized that someone was sitting next to me. Startled, I stared into the beautiful face of a tall, strong man who was wearing clothes that appeared to be made out of white light. Gingerly, I reached my hand towards the shining cloth but didn't feel a thing. Was this my guardian angel? He smiled and I felt immensely comforted. He told me that Jimmy was okay and that I shouldn't worry. The angel also told me I didn't need to be afraid to eat. As he spoke, warmth flooded through my body. I grabbed my spoon, devoured the oatmeal, and ran to the kitchen to ask for more. After I finished eating, the young man disappeared, and I never saw him again.

"I never told anyone about the angel. I couldn't bear to be robbed of my joy through someone else's disbelief. That day I knew that the Father of the fatherless had swept into my life and that he would care for me. Talking to God became as natural as breathing. A while later I was even able to visit Jimmy. He was finally being adopted. I had memorized every freckle on my brother's face, so dear was he to me. But I was no longer afraid to live without him. God would watch over me so much better than any big brother ever could.

"To my joy, I was later adopted by a couple who provided a loving, nurturing home for me. That day with the angel was the turning point of my life. No longer was I a little girl without family or friends. I had an angel to watch over me and a Father in heaven who would never fail me or forsake me."

Father, you care about the widow and the orphan. You are a father to the fatherless. When I feel desolate, remind me of how close you are. Help me to understand that you are full of compassion.

THE ANGEL
AND THE ACCIDENT

If you make the Most High your dwelling —
    even the LORD, who is my refuge —
then no harm will befall you....
For he will command his angels concerning you
    to guard you in all your ways;
they will lift you up in their hands,
    so that you will not strike your foot against a stone.

Psalm 91:9–12

Sharyl Smith was a student nurse who had a reputation for queasiness. She had walked out, passed out, and been dragged out of operating rooms because she couldn't stand the sight and smells of surgery. You wouldn't have pegged her as a hero at the scene of a gory accident. But she was.

Sharyl was on her way to school one day when she rounded a hill in her car. In the line of traffic ahead she saw a large truck crossing an intersection. Suddenly it appeared to "break apart, like a train derailing." Pieces of it caught fire and landed on the side of the road ahead of her. Sharyl pulled over. The cab had tumbled into a ditch, and she could see the driver slumped over the steering wheel, a wash of blood obscuring his face.

Sharyl screamed for help, but people seemed paralyzed, gaping at the wreck. Someone shouted that the truck was about to explode.

Then she saw it. Gasoline was gushing out of the tank onto the ground. The cab was already on fire and so was the grass in the ditch. She hesitated for a moment and then ran toward the truck.

"If no one would help me, then I'd just have to get him out alone. I would rather die than stand there and watch that man die. As I ran through the fire to the truck, I felt as though an invisible bubble was wrapped around me, protecting me. When I opened the cab door, fire shot out toward me, yet I was not burned. The ruptured gas tank poured gasoline toward my feet, making a strange sound as it poured onto the ground."

Terrified lest the truck blow up, she dragged the limp body of the man partly out of the cab. His pants were already on fire, but she couldn't seem to pull him clear of the wreck. Desperately, she prayed, "Dear God, please help us!"

Suddenly a man appeared at her side. The driver's foot had been lodged in the door, and he lifted it free. Then he smothered the remaining flames on the injured man's clothes, and together they dragged him to safety.

By then the police had arrived with an ambulance. At the hospital, Sharyl was given some scrubs to change into. As she removed the white ivory cross from around her neck, she realized it was covered with blood. Alone in the room, she opened the window wide, gazed out at the blue sky, and thanked God for his mercy.

Against all odds she was alive and so was the driver of that ill-fated truck. Later, she learned that he had made a full recovery.

Sharyl's story was told in *The Journal of Christian Nursing* (Summer 1993 issue, p. 22). Because of her experience, she knows there was more to this story than one woman's act of bravery. "I have no explanation for the bubble of protection that I felt while in the fiery ditch. I know the soles of my rubber shoes were melted; flames shot out of the cab directly toward my head when I opened the door; not one hair on my head was even singed, not one burn did I acquire. I am convinced that God sent an angel to protect me that fateful day.... I do not know why the accident happened.... I only know that I believe in divine intervention. I believe in miracles."

Jesus, after two thousand years, your words still haunt us: "Greater love has no one than this, that he lay down his life for his friends" (John 15:13). Give us the courage to live them, no matter the cost.

FACE TO FACE

For I tell you that their [the little ones'] angels in heaven always see the face of my Father in heaven.

Matthew 18:10

The Bible tells us that no one can see God's face and live. Moses, whose relationship with God was one of extraordinary intimacy, begged God to show him his glory. But God replied, "You cannot see my face, for no one may see me and live.... You will see my back; but my face must not be seen" (Exodus 33:20, 23). Even so, when Moses talked with God, his own face shone so brilliantly that he had to cover it in the presence of others. His fellow Israelites could not bear even the reflected glory of God.

We can only imagine what it must be like to see God's face—to perceive his beauty, his power, his holiness, and his love. Though we differ in our capacity to see God, none of us yet have the ability to know him as he knows us. It's as though God is telling us that it's still too dangerous, like trying to pour Niagara Falls into a thimble. We would be utterly crushed and destroyed.

Yet Jesus tells us that angels in heaven continually enjoy face-to-face communion with God. Maybe that's why they make such great guardians. They know how overwhelmingly attractive God is, and they are not seduced, as we are, into making idols out of lesser desires. Unlike the fallen angels, they know the foolishness of choosing less when you can have more.

How can you cherish a lie when you live in the presence of truth? How can you become anxious about the future when you've seen how things turn out? How can you try to control your life and the lives of those around you when you understand the depth of God's wisdom and the greatness of his power? Why would you choose fool's gold when you know where the mother lode is?

Lord, whenever I catch a glimpse of you, I long for more. Purge my soul of its darkness, that no shadows will blind me to your presence. Open my eyes that I may see what angels see.

LADDER OF ANGELS

*He [Jacob] dreamed that there was a ladder set up on the
earth, the top of it reaching to heaven; and the angels of God
were ascending and descending on it. And the LORD stood
beside him and said, "I am the LORD, the God of Abraham
your father and the God of Isaac."*

Genesis 28:12–13 NRSV

When I was a child, one of my favorite television programs
was *The Twilight Zone*. Its eerie stories, packed with surprising twists and turns, always piqued my imagination. Each program
told the tale of unsuspecting people who were about to embark
on an extraordinary adventure. Without warning, they would find
themselves in a different world, not unlike their own but somehow
strangely different. They had crossed over into that territory of the
mind known as "the twilight zone."

Jacob had a dream that transported him into his own version
of the twilight zone. He was on his way to Haran, the hometown
of his grandfather Abraham. When night drew on, he slept under
the starry sky with only a stone for a pillow and dreamed of angels
climbing up and down a ladder connecting heaven and earth.
When he awoke, he was terrified and exclaimed to himself, "Surely
the LORD is in this place—and I did not know it!... This is none
other than the house of God, and this is the gate of heaven" (Genesis 28:16–17 NRSV).

The ladder in Jacob's dream symbolized the connection that exists between heaven and earth. The angels move up and down the ladder, bearing our needs to God and carrying his provision to us. Jacob's strange dream, however, awaited its full interpretation for hundreds of years, until Jesus said, "I tell you, you will see heaven opened and the angels of God ascending and descending upon the Son of Man" (John 1:50 NRSV). Hitherto, the link between heaven and earth had been damaged by our disobedience. In Jesus, it was fully repaired. He is the link, the ladder, the gate between the throne of God and his people on earth.

Astonishing as this is, it's not the end of the story. The infinite distance between heaven and earth, between a holy God and sinful human beings, has been bridged by a Savior who actually lives within his people. Incredibly, this means that the ladder to heaven exists, not in some faraway place, but right inside us. If we belong to Christ, we can echo Jacob's surprise and exclaim about our own souls, "How awesome is this place! This is none other than the house of God; this is the gate of heaven."

Father, your love is strong and persistent. Thank you the gift of life in your Son. Help me to honor his presence within me by living in a way that acknowledges his goodness.

2

Now You See Them,
Now You Don't

Angels don't submit to litmus tests, testify in court, or slide
under a microscope for examination. Thus, their existence cannot
be "proved" by the guidelines we humans usually use. To know one,
perhaps, requires a willingness to suspend judgment, to open
ourselves to possibilities we've only dreamed about.

Joan Wester Anderson, *Where Angels Walk*

Why do some people see angels while others see nothing? In one incident described in Scripture, a donkey sees an angel blocking the path ahead while its rider is oblivious to the angel's presence (Numbers 22:21–35). Perhaps the answer lies with both God and us. First, the Lord has reasons we may never understand for opening the eyes of one person and shutting the eyes of another. Second, perhaps some of us have the kind of simple faith that invites the angels to show up.

One of my favorite pastimes as a child was to spend hours with my older brother and sister hunting for turtles. With nets in hand, we'd roam the lake on which we lived looking for pointy snouts to break the surface here and there. As soon as we spotted one, the chase was on. They were quick, but we were quicker.

Part of the problem with catching turtles is that they blend in so well with their natural habitat, making them difficult to see. But we loved these creatures and knew their habits and their hiding places. We told ourselves that we had developed "turtle eyes," the ability to see turtles where other people only saw reeds and logs and murky water.

I suspect that some people have developed similar skills when it comes to spotting angels. They've developed "angel eyes." They are sensitive to the variety of ways that God works in our world and are open to the possibility of miracles.

I confess that I have never actually seen an angel. But as I reflect upon my life, I sense the traces of their presence. As you read these brief meditations, take some time to think about your own life. Maybe, just maybe, the angels were at work and you didn't even know it.

OPEN OUR EYES

Elisha prayed, "O LORD, open his eyes so he may see." Then the LORD opened the servant's eyes, and he looked and saw the hills full of horses and chariots of fire all around Elisha.

2 Kings 6:17

Sometimes we feel surrounded by trouble and difficulty, beset on every side by problems of one kind or another. This was the case with Elisha, an Old Testament prophet, who had angered one of the local kings. He and his servant awoke one morning to find their city surrounded by an army intent on capturing them. They were outgunned, outmanned, and outmaneuvered. It must have looked like the last stand of Butch Cassidy and the Sundance Kid. But it wasn't.

Elisha's calm counterbalanced his servant's terror. The prophet saw something no one else did. Though it looked as if Elisha was outnumbered, his enemies were actually surrounded by a vast angelic host. Elisha prayed that God would open the eyes of his frightened servant so that he could perceive what was really going on—that God had planned a heavenly ambush to protect them.

Elisha's story tells us that some things can only be seen through the eyes of faith. But faith is something that does not come naturally to us. We want to taste, touch, and see for ourselves before we will believe.

A few years ago, a friend of mine was consumed by anxiety for her future. As she voiced her apprehensions, she said something that sums up our struggle to believe: "If I could only see what's going to happen, I could trust God for it." But the point of faith is that we need it *because* we can't see into the future.

My friend was making the same mistake I have often made. She was identifying faith with a certain kind of outcome. If things would work out as she hoped they would, then she would believe. But our faith will fail us if we tie it to a set of circumstances. It will become more like positive thinking than real faith. Instead, the faith that nourishes us involves trust in Someone rather than something — in the character of a God who is both loving and powerful enough to save us. God does not ask us to blindly trust him. Instead, he reveals himself through Scripture and through our own experience, to convince us that he is trustworthy.

God may or may not send an army of angels to rescue us, but we can be certain he will provide for us. We know that he sees around corners we don't even know exist. The more we trust him to provide, the more our faith will grow. We may not have supernatural visions of the kind that Elisha had, but we will develop keen spiritual insight as our faith increases. Angels or no angels, we will know without a doubt that our God is faithful.

Lord, sometimes I wish you would hand me a crystal ball so that I could read the future. But I know you would much rather take me by surprise. Help me to realize that my security comes from placing my trust in you, not from knowing what's going to happen the day after tomorrow for the rest of my life.

Sometimes Angels Don't Fly

It was no messenger or angel but his presence that saved them.
Isaiah 63:9 NRSV

My father was a fighter pilot during World War II. He flew combat missions for the Air Force in Italy, France, and Germany. As a child, I enjoyed hearing that he had named his fighter bomber, a Thunderbolt P47, Sweetieface, his nickname for my mother, to whom he was engaged during the war.

A few years ago, he told me a story about his wartime experience that sent chills down my spine. It was April 1945 and the war in Europe was nearly over. He was leading an armed reconnaissance mission in central Germany when his squadron spotted an enemy airfield. They were later ordered back to the area to destroy the field, which they did.

"We bombed the hangars and strafed the field until nothing much was left. So many aircraft were destroyed that day that our commanding officer nominated us for a presidential citation. To document the success of the mission, I was eventually sent back to the field with two other men to photograph the wreckage.

"Once on the ground we realized that a few of the planes were still in pretty good shape. One of these was an ME109 Fighter. We thought it would make a nice prize for the Air Force, so we decided to fly it back to our airfield. I climbed into the cockpit, but when

I turned the ignition, nothing happened. The battery was dead, so we left the plane where it stood. Later, I discovered that it had been booby-trapped with explosives in the wheel wells. Had that plane started, I would have been blown to bits."

I couldn't help but think about how incredibly different things would have been had the battery worked that day. My father would never have returned; his five children would never have been born; my mother would have married another man; you would never have read this book.... It's hard for me to stop thinking about the implications. Thank God for a mechanical failure. Or was it a failure, I wonder. Had God himself preserved my father's life for all that was yet to be? You may call it a coincidence, but I believe it was Providence at work. It may not have been an angel, but then again...

Father, I marvel at how well you care for us. Thank you for watching over every member of my family—my father and mother, my spouse, my children. There isn't a moment in our lives when your loving eye does not see us. You even number the hairs on our heads. Help me to remember that when I start to fret and worry over those I love the most.

THE LITTLE GIRL
AND THE ANGEL

⥲

One day Jesus was praying in a certain place. When he finished, one of his disciples said to him, "Lord, teach us to pray, just as John taught his disciples."

Luke 11:1

One of June Scouten's favorite prayers is the Lord's Prayer, the same one Jesus taught his disciples two thousand years ago. When you hear her story, you'll know why.

"I was six years old when it happened. My family attended a Methodist church in Washington, D.C., and one of the requirements in my Sunday school class was to learn the Lord's Prayer. I was good at a lot of things, but memorization wasn't one of them. My mother could remember anything she put her mind to, so she couldn't understand why it was so hard for me. In fact, I've always been that way. I could ad lib my way out of any kind of trouble, but couldn't memorize a page of text to save my life. No matter how hard I tried to remember the prayer, I couldn't keep the words straight.

"Saturday night came and I still couldn't recite the prayer all the way through. I was worried because I wanted to do well, but how could I? As I was climbing into bed, I said: 'God, I need some help remembering this prayer. Please do something.' I drifted off into the most wonderful dream. Someone very beautiful came into my room and took me in his arms. I felt him lifting me and then transporting me through the air to a strange place. All the while, I felt safe and warm, not at all frightened by the experience. I remember seeing light, pretty colors and then being brought into the presence of someone else.

"Then I began to feel very small and thought to myself that I was in the presence of a Great One. Don't ask me why I thought that, I just did. Yet I still felt very much at peace. Then this person, I believe it was Jesus, spoke to me. He simply said the Lord's Prayer very deliberately and clearly one time through. Then I woke up.

"From that moment, I knew the prayer perfectly. I felt relieved and at peace, knowing I would be able to recite it at church. I don't know why God heard the prayer of a worried little girl, but I believe he sent an angel to me that night to bring me into his presence so he could teach me the prayer of his heart."

Our Father, who art in heaven, hallowed be thy name. Thy kingdom come, thy will be done, on earth as it is in heaven. Give us this day our daily bread, and forgive us our trespasses as we forgive those who trespass against us. And lead us not into temptation, but deliver us from evil. For thine is the kingdom, the power, and the glory, forever. Amen.

THWARTED

Then the LORD opened Balaam's eyes, and he saw the angel of the LORD standing in the road with his sword drawn.... The angel of the LORD asked him, "Why have you beaten your donkey these three times? I have come here to oppose you because your path is a reckless one before me."

Numbers 22:31–32

Balaam had prophetic gifts. That's why the King of Moab had summoned him. He wanted Balaam to place a curse on the Israelites who were encamped nearby. On his way to the king, Balaam encountered a fierce angel who blocked his path. His donkey saw the angel, though Balaam didn't. When the animal refused to budge, Balaam kept hitting the beast to get him to move. Then God opened Balaam's eyes and the angel spoke to him.

This story tells us that angels sometimes block our path because we are heading in the wrong direction. That's what happened to me a few years ago. I was working to secure a business deal that a number of other companies were also pursuing. I tried everything I could think of, but one obstacle after another kept popping up. I was frustrated, but refused to give up. Persistence is one of my professional virtues. It is also one of my vices.

Finally, though, I did stop pursuing the matter. Later, circumstances made it abundantly clear that it would have been a mistake to proceed. I couldn't see it at the time, but I now believe that God was blocking the path to keep my company from getting involved in something that would have blown up in its face. Perhaps if I had asked God to show me what was going on, I would have wasted less time and energy. I simply didn't see the situation clearly. I thought I knew the best course of action, and I tenaciously pursued it.

Paul's first letter to the Corinthians puts it like this: "For now we see in a mirror, dimly, but then we will see face to face. Now I know only in part; then I will know fully, even as I have been fully known" (1 Corinthians 13:12 NRSV). In this world our vision is blurred. Without God's help, we cannot tell which direction to pursue. Unless he opens our eyes, we simply will not be able to see things as they are. We may even pray against the work of Satan, only to find that we are opposing God himself.

Perhaps you are feeling thwarted in some way. You may be involved in a relationship that is going nowhere, a business deal that has soured, a ministry that is fraught with trouble. How do you know if you are under spiritual attack or if an angel of the Lord is trying to tell you something? Rather than assuming you know what God's will is, stop and ask him for wisdom. Pray that he will help you discern what is really going on. Is this a situation that calls for endurance and perseverance, or is God trying to point out another direction for you or your ministry?

Resist the temptation to keep beating your particular donkey, to force him to tread the path you have chosen. Ask humbly for God to guide you, and he will show you if one of his angels is blocking the path ahead. If he is, you dare not risk going forward.

Father, you have eyes that can see to infinity while I cannot even see what's around the next corner. Forgive me for the times I have stubbornly persisted in the wrong way. Make me more sensitive to your angels and to your Holy Spirit, so that I will at least have the sense of Balaam's donkey to stand still and listen, to allow you to turn me around and head me in another direction.

Was It Really an Angel?

There the angel of the LORD appeared to [Moses] in flames of fire from within a bush.... "Do not come any closer," God said. "Take off your sandals, for the place where you are standing is holy ground." Then he said, "I am the God of your father, the God of Abraham, the God of Isaac and the God of Jacob."

Exodus 3:2, 5–6

Sometimes the Bible describes God as an "angel of the Lord." This is the phrase used in Moses' encounter with the burning bush. In this case, God makes himself known. Some theologians believe that this phrase always refers to God, rather than an actual angel. Whatever the case, it raises a question: How do you know whether something is the work of an angel or of the Holy Spirit? The answer is that most of the time you don't know. But does it really matter? Angels, after all, merely carry out God's plans. They do so joyfully since their wills are one with God's, but he's the One with the big ideas. They simply see to the details.

The truth is that God has an infinite number of ways of caring for us. Often, he even chooses human beings rather than angels to convey a message of his love. Here's how he used a friend of mine one day.

Briefcase in hand, the collar of his trench coat turned up against the morning chill, Mark stood waiting for a city bus. He couldn't shake the feeling that he was supposed to share the gospel with someone on the bus that day. "Finally I shot up a quick prayer acknowledging that I was willing to try if only God would show me whom to talk to and what to say," Mark explained.

"I sat down next to an elderly man who looked as though he'd seen better days. Try as I might, I just couldn't get the guy to talk. Finally, I pulled out a small New Testament and randomly opened it to Romans 5:1 – 2. Then I noticed that he held a pocket New Testament in his hands. I asked him about it, and he told me that someone had given it to him, with the suggestion that he investigate Christianity. I read the passage from Romans aloud: 'Therefore, since we have been justified through faith, we have peace with God through our Lord Jesus Christ, through whom we have gained access by faith into this grace in which we now stand.' We talked for a few moments longer about what it means to have peace with God. Then I gave him my phone number in case he had any questions. When we parted, the old man turned to me with a smile and said, 'Well, you really have brightened my day.'

"I was out that evening, but my wife fielded a phone call for me that neither one of us will ever forget. It was the man on the bus. 'I need to thank your husband for something he said to me today. At first I didn't want to have anything to do with him. I even thought he might be a federal agent. He looked so clean-cut, with his trench coat and briefcase. But then he pulled out that Bible. Do you know that I was on my way home to commit suicide?' he told Sarah. 'Your husband's words about God changed my mind. I owe him a great deal.'

"I was astonished when Sarah told me the story that night. I didn't have a clue about what was going through that man's mind as we sat side by side on the bus that morning. But God knew. He knows what's in all our minds. That day he gave me an inclination and the grace to follow it."

Mark had simply listened to an interior prompting, a gentle whisper from the Holy Spirit. He was willing to risk embarrassment on the chance that God had something in mind. Mark spoke of what God had done in his own life, and his words sparked in that desperate man a new hope and a reason to live.

Mark is as human as anyone I know. He didn't announce himself in a burning bush (or bus, in this case) or with a trumpet blast, but he was definitely a messenger sent from heaven, an angel of flesh and blood, ready to do God's will.

You and I may never see an angel, but we know that they exist and that they work unceasingly on our behalf. Whether God is at work through his angels, directly through his Holy Spirit, or through us, doesn't really matter. What matters is that God loves us and finds an infinite number of ways to reassure us of that love.

> *"I am a link in a chain, a bond of connection between persons. God has not created me for naught. I shall do good, I shall do his work. I shall be an angel of peace, a preacher of truth in my own place while not intending it—if I do but keep his commandments."*
>
> John Henry Newman

3

Angels to Guard Us

❦

Angels where'er we go,
Attend our steps whate'er betide.
With watchful care their charge attend,
And evil turn aside.

Charles Wesley

We live in a dangerous world. At any moment our future could be erased by a heart attack, an accident, or a knife in the hands of an intruder. Worse than our anxiety for our own lives is our concern for our children. They seem defenseless against a predatory world, and our power to protect them is often inadequate.

Fortunately, God has not left them or us without recourse. One of the ways he protects us is through angelic guardians. Though Christians differ as to whether each of us has been assigned a personal guardian angel, most agree that angels watch over us in one way or another.

In fact, Scripture is replete with the feats of guardian angels. They blind prison guards, enabling believers to escape. They break chains as though they were snapping rubber bands. They transport people from one place to another. They impart courage in a moment of terror. They confound armies with their fierceness. In the world today they often work in hidden ways to preserve a life, to protect a church, and even to save a nation. Always, they work to carry out God's will. Perhaps their greatest accomplishments have more to do with protecting men and women from spiritual rather than mere material harm.

When you are tempted to feel afraid, for yourself or for your children, remember that you have the advantage of angels, powerful supernatural beings who are constantly watching over you. Though you do not see them, they are standing by to place a loving arm between you and danger. Take a moment and ask God to increase your confidence in his provision and to help you cooperate with the angels so that they can take care of you with joy.

An Angel on Board

*For last night there stood by me an angel of the God to whom
I belong and whom I worship, and he said, "Do not be afraid,
Paul; you must stand before the emperor; and indeed God has
granted safety to all those who are sailing with you." So keep
up your courage, men, for I have faith in God that it will be
exactly as I have been told. But we will have to run aground
on some island.*

Acts 27:23–26 NRSV

Paul had been placed under arrest in Jerusalem after a riot broke
out in the temple in opposition to his preaching. He was now
aboard an Alexandrian ship bound for Rome, where he was to
make his defense before the emperor. Soldiers were also on board
to convey Paul and a number of other prisoners to Rome.

En route to a safe haven in Crete, where crew and passengers
planned to wait out the dangerous winter months, the ship ran
afoul in a violent Nor'easter. The storm was so ferocious that the
entire cargo and the ship's tackle had to be thrown overboard to
lighten the load. For several days the forbidding sky refused to
reveal a hint of sun or stars.

Finally, when hope had become nothing more than a dead
man's dream, Paul told the others about his encounter with the
angel. Like them, Paul had been terrified by the storm. But the
angel calmed his fears and assured him that God would fulfill his
purpose for Paul: he would arrive safely in Rome, where he would

appear before the emperor and witness to his faith. Not only that, God had granted safe passage to everyone on board.

The angel imparted new courage to Paul. In turn, Paul was able to encourage the others. He was certain that the outcome would be exactly as the angel had told him.

However, some of the crew members failed to share Paul's faith. A few days later they tried to jump ship in order to save themselves. The soldiers were little better. They planned to kill the prisoners in the event of a shipwreck, lest any escape.

Even so, events proved Paul right about the angel's words. Everything happened exactly as the angel said it would. The ship ran against a reef and broke apart, but every single passenger escaped to safety on the island of Malta. And Paul was later transported to Rome to plead his case.

Paul talks about his heavenly encourager as an "angel of the God to whom I belong." He knew that his life and his future belonged in God's own hands. The same is true for every man and woman who loves God. Like Paul, we can expect that God will provide supernaturally for us. When we find ourselves at sea, not knowing which direction to turn, or when we discover ourselves the victim of some kind of disaster or shipwreck, we can echo the psalmist's words: "I cry to God Most High, to God who fulfills his purpose for me" (Psalm 57:2 NRSV).

For God does have a plan and purpose for each one of us, no matter how stormy our circumstances. Like Paul we can find courage in the word that God speaks to us. And as we grow in courage we can, in turn, encourage those around us. Perhaps the God to whom we belong will send an angel to stand by us in our time of greatest need.

My Father, sometimes I feel as though enormous waves will swallow me whole. I'm frightened and confused, and yet I know that you love and care for me. Even though my plans may fail and my circumstances may end in shipwreck, I know that I can cry out to you and that you will yet fulfill your purposes for me.

THE TODDLER
AND THE ANGEL

‹⁓›

For he will command his angels concerning you
*   to guard you in all your ways;*
they will lift you up in their hands,
*   so that you will not strike your foot against a stone.*

Psalm 91:11 – 12

When I was a teenager, I spoke like a teenager, I thought like a teenager, and I *drove* like a teenager. In fact, I loved driving my mother's Thunderbird convertible at top speed, both in town and on the highway. I was young. I was indestructible. I was foolish.

One July morning I pulled into the driveway of a friend's home. We had planned a day at the beach, and the weather was cooperating perfectly. We were excited to get going as quickly as possible, to catch all the rays that were to be caught. She climbed in, and I was just about to gun the engine into reverse, in my characteristically enthusiastic way. Suddenly I heard screams and shouts issuing from the house next door. As I turned to look, I saw the neighbors running frantically in our direction.

The object of their distress soon became apparent. A blond-haired toddler, perched on a tricycle, had been blissfully clinging to the rear bumper of my car, unaware of his peril. I could not possibly have seen him as I prepared to back out of the driveway. One moment later, and this little boy would have been crushed beneath the wheels of the car.

I have little doubt that this toddler's guardian angel was on duty that day. And perhaps my angel had a hand in things too. The horror of that moment would have haunted me for the rest of my life—to have been the unwitting cause of a young child's death. I have thanked God many times since that he spared me that particular sorrow.

Who knows how many times you may have been saved from some tragedy or other by your guardian angel? Some of our angels, it's true, have to rise to the occasion more often than others. My father, who has had his share of close encounters, thinks he may have worn out several guardian angels in the course of his life. (I suspect that his simply took a few well-deserved vacations, rather than opting for early retirement.)

The point, of course, is not to see who can make their guardian angels run fastest and jump highest. It's simply to thank God for his loving care for us, "for commanding his angels to guard us in all our ways."

Father, how many times have you saved me from some catastrophe that I didn't even know was threatening? How many times did you send an angel to my rescue without my suspecting it? Thank you, Lord, that you make your angels winds and your servants flames of fire, heavenly servants to keep us safe.

A MIRACLE
IN JOHANNESBURG

~~~

*See, I am sending an angel ahead of you to guard you along
the way and to bring you to the place I have prepared.*
                                                    Exodus 23:20

Chris and Jan were in a crowded airport in Johannesburg,
South Africa, on a hot Friday afternoon. It had been a trying day. They had missed their flight to neighboring Zimbabwe
and had been wait-listed for the next. Suddenly, tickets were issued
and loudspeakers announced that the flight would be departing
momentarily. All passengers should proceed immediately to the
gate.

As they hastily gathered their things in order to board the
flight, they found that hundreds of other passengers were hurrying
in the same direction. "There must have been a hundred people
cramming down the swift-moving escalator, with a huge crowd
coming right behind them," explained Chris. "In front of us was
a short, plump Greek-looking lady carrying bags that were much
too heavy for her. She was so loaded down that she couldn't hang
onto the handrails.

"Suddenly, she fell backwards on the steps of the escalator. She
couldn't possibly get up by herself and, though we tried, we couldn't
help her. Things were happening very rapidly. In a moment this
poor lady would reach the bottom of the escalator and the rest of us

would pitch forward on top of her, crushing the life out of her. In turn, I knew that we and others might be crushed to death by the mass of bodies behind us. Jan and I both cried out, 'Lord, help us!' and the most amazing thing happened. Suddenly this stout woman literally floated in the air and stood up on her feet. Her bags were neatly by her side, and we made it to our flight.

"Jan and I both sensed the angels that had lifted her up. We know for a fact that what happened was a supernatural event. We cried out to God and he heard us. He saved many lives that day, including ours."

The Bible tells us that the Lord holds us in the palm of his hand, that underneath are the everlasting arms of a mighty God. In the frenzy of that experience, Chris and Jan never got to talk things over with the woman who had been lifted to her feet. If they had, perhaps she would have described strong arms holding her and sending her safely on her way.

Father, I never know when an ordinary situation may suddenly turn threatening, but you do. Whether my peril is physical, spiritual, or emotional, I know that your strong arms and the arms of your mighty angels are there to hold me up when I am too weak to stand. Thank you, God, for raising me whenever I fall.

Unchained by an Angel

~⚕~

The night before Herod was to bring him to trial, Peter was sleeping between two soldiers, bound with two chains, and sentries stood guard at the entrance. Suddenly an angel of the Lord appeared and a light shone in the cell. He struck Peter on the side and woke him up. "Quick, get up!" he said, and the chains fell off Peter's wrists.

Acts 12:6–7

If you have ever been to Rome, you may have visited St. Peter in Chains, a church that claims to display the chains mentioned in this passage. Whether these are Peter's chains I cannot say. But this church reminds us that Peter really was freed by an angel while under heavy guard in Jerusalem.

Shortly before Peter was arrested, King Herod Agrippa had put the apostle James to death. The people seemed pleased by this execution, so Herod grew bolder and arrested Peter. He handed him over to four squads of soldiers who were to guard him night and day. When the believers in the city heard the disastrous news, they prayed fervently for Peter's release.

One night, while Peter was sleeping, flanked on either side by guards, his angel came and nudged him awake. The next day Peter would have been brought out to the people, presumably for execution. But now the chains literally fell off Peter's wrists, and he walked out of prison and into the city a free man.

It took only one guardian angel to hoodwink four squads of soldiers who were standing guard. Herod became so infuriated when he heard about Peter's escape that he executed the guards.

Peter himself could hardly believe what had happened. He went straight to the house of some believers in the city. What occurred next is one of the more humorous incidents related in the New Testament. When Peter knocked on the door, a maid named Rhoda answered. She was so excited to see him that she left him standing at the door and ran back to tell the others, who promptly told her she was out of her mind. They had prayed for Peter, but they could not believe that God had really answered their prayers. Meanwhile, fugitive Peter stood on the steps, desperately hoping that someone would let him in.

From Peter's story, we learn that our angels possess far greater power than the powers of evil that threaten us. We also learn that God heard the prayers of his people, despite their little faith. God had a plan for Peter and for his people that would not be subverted by any evil plan of his enemy. He allowed James to suffer a martyr's death. But Peter he spared for another purpose, through the ministry of an angel.

The gospel is in chains in many parts of the world today, and many believers suffer as a result. We need to pray especially for those who are heralds of the good news, that God will send his angels to open prison doors so that many more people might come to know his mercy and his forgiveness. No matter how strong the opposition, God can send powerful angels who with a touch can overcome all resistance.

Lord, I know that many of your people are suffering and being martyred for their faith all over the world. I pray that you will confuse and confound every earthly and spiritual tyrant who attempts to suppress the good news. Send your angels to empty out the prisons where my brothers and sisters are held and enable them to preach your Word with even greater power.

A DISTRESSING DREAM

... and the angel of his presence saved them.
In his love and mercy he redeemed them;
he lifted them up and carried them
all the days of old.

Isaiah 63:9

Marilynn Carlson Webber, with her husband, William D. Webber, is the author of *A Rustle of Angels*. Despite having written about angels, she never laid eyes on one until the summer of 1993. That's when she had a vision of angels—in a distressing dream in the middle of the night.

"I had written an article about angels for *Guideposts* magazine, which resulted in an astonishing flood of mail from all over the world—more than 8,500 letters. You can imagine what my mailman must have thought—perhaps I had invented a cure for cancer or maybe I was selling drugs through the mail.

"Hundreds of letters contained such beautiful accounts of angelic visitations that they filled me with wonder and longing. I wanted to see the shining creatures people so movingly described. So one day I asked God to let me see an angel before I died. I didn't know whether he would, but I knew it wouldn't hurt to ask. Then I forgot about my prayer. Several months later, I dreamed of four angels who looked nothing like the magnificent angels I longed to see.

"Dressed in long black robes, their faces were downcast and even their wings looked black. They were angels all right, but not the ones I expected. I remember saying in my dream, 'Lord, these aren't the right ones. There must be some mistake.'

"I could tell by the way they carried themselves that they were in mourning. Though I felt intimidated, I summoned the courage to ask one of the angels why they were all so sad. His answer frightened me: 'We're sad because you're dying. If something is not done soon, you will die.'

"When I woke up, I recounted the dream to my husband, Bill. As I was telling him about it, I began to experience pain in my abdomen for the first time. Though I have always been a reluctant patient and hadn't been to a doctor in years, we decided I should call a doctor that day. Before, when I had phoned the Loma Linda Clinic, I was told there was a two-year waiting period for new patients. But that morning Bill got on the phone, insistent that someone examine me.

"'Why is it so urgent your wife see a doctor?' the nurse inquired.

"Bill knew it sounded crazy but decided to tell her about the dream. She excused herself, saying she needed to put him on hold for a moment. Fully expecting the next voice he heard to belong to a psychiatrist, he was surprised when the nurse returned to say the doctor would see me the following Wednesday.

"Tests confirmed I was suffering from ovarian cancer. My doctor had heard about my dream and was amazed I had heeded it. 'You have a lot to be thankful for,' he told me. 'I see so many women who wait too long before seeking treatment. By the time they know something's wrong, it's often too late. Pain isn't a symptom in the early stages of ovarian cancer.'

"Surgery was set for September 2, 1993, at the Loma Linda University Medical Center. The doctor warned that I was a high-risk patient and would need to be in intensive care for several days after the surgery.

"Of course I am a great believer in prayer, so I called friends and asked them to intercede. Expecting to be on edge the morning of the surgery, I was surprised to feel completely at peace. After a few hours in the recovery room, I was wheeled back to my hospital room. I had come through with flying colors. No need for intensive care. No need even for chemotherapy or any other follow-up treatments. The doctors felt confident they had caught the cancer in time.

"Why had I experienced pain the morning of the dream when pain isn't a symptom of the disease? Wasn't it to emphasize the message of my dream? I had prayed to see angels of dazzling beauty. Instead, I saw four angels dressed in black. Not the angels I wanted to see, but the angels I needed to see in order to experience God's healing touch."

Father, thank you for the amazing ways you guard and protect us. Help us to heed your voice.

4

ANGELS WITH A MESSAGE

❧

It is the province of knowledge to speak
and it is the privilege of wisdom to listen.

Oliver Wendell Holmes Sr.

Angels carry out a variety of supernatural roles in the structure of the universe. Their favorite seems to be that of messenger. In fact, the most frequent mention of them in the Bible is as messengers. The word *angel* derives from the Greek *angelos*, which in turn translates the Hebrew *mal'ak*, meaning "messenger."

The angels aren't merely heavenly mailmen, carrying love letters, special offers, and dunning notices from heaven to earth. Their role has much greater dignity. More like ambassadors than message boys, they represent the very presence and intentions of God himself.

Perhaps that's why they often seem to terrify people, who experience the same kind of awe that they might in the presence of a holy God. Frequently the angel's first words are "do not be afraid." The angel Gabriel, whose primary role seemed to be that of messenger, told both Zechariah and Mary not to be afraid when he told them about the forthcoming births of John the Baptist and Jesus.

Do the angels still speak? Or are they silent now that the canon of Scripture has been closed? Certainly, angels can neither add nor subtract to the revelation of the Bible, but I believe they still convey messages from heaven to earth. Often, what we think of as mere coincidences may really be aspects of providence at work in our lives.

Remember the time you failed to notice an oncoming car until it was nearly too late? What caused you to look up just in time? Or perhaps a friend called not knowing that you desperately needed to hear from her. Maybe someone else said something that addressed a secret need in your life. Could the angels have been speaking, whispering a message from God himself?

If we have ears to hear, God will surely speak to us, and sometimes he will even use an angel to tell us of his mercy and guide us along the way.

An Angel
and Two Miracles

Greetings, favored one! The Lord is with you.... Do not be afraid, Mary, for you have found favor with God.

Luke 1:28, 30 NRSV

With these startling words, the angel Gabriel announced to Mary that she would give birth to a son who would inherit the throne of the great King David.

Not long afterward, Mary visited her cousin Elizabeth, who lived in the hill country of Judea. It was a meeting of opposite miracles—a young girl who had conceived a child without ever having slept with a man and a barren old woman whose womb had suddenly swollen with life.

Elizabeth's greeting rang out to Mary, "Blessed are you among women, and blessed is the fruit of your womb" (Luke 1:42).

How strange and wonderful, to be called "favored" by an angel and then "blessed among women" by Elizabeth, the barren one who herself had been labeled "unblessed" all her married life!

Yet I wonder if these greetings came back to haunt Mary years later. Did the terrible irony of these words "blessed are you" pierce her soul as she watched her son carry his cross to Calvary, the hill of his unspeakable agony? Did the angel's promise that her child would be called the "Son of the Most High" ring mockingly in her ears as she stared at the bitter notice nailed to the wood above his head: "Jesus of Nazareth, King of the Jews"?

Was she tempted to think, "If this is what it means to be blessed, I don't want your blessing, God!"

We don't know. The Scriptures are silent. We can only imagine. Yet we do know that Mary was found with the disciples in the upper room when the Holy Spirit descended on them like fire. Like them, she was praying and seeking God, no doubt searching her own soul but still clinging to his promises.

Mary's tenacity in the face of confusion, anxiety, disappointment, and terrible grief can be a source of comfort and strength. Have you ever received a message from God, a promise or a blessing, only to find that his definition of blessing or his timing and yours were out of sync? Mary may have wondered, as you have wondered, whether she really heard God or only imagined it. Perhaps she thought she had entertained delusions of grandeur. Why would God send an angelic messenger to her, a nobody from Nazareth? Yet she knew that he had.

You may have sensed the presence of an angel, whispering to you of God's love and his faithfulness. Resist the temptation to let go of whatever God has said to you through his word. Admit that you may not fully understand what he has spoken or promised, but ask him to show you and to give you faith as his word unfolds. Don't become discouraged if you don't feel blessed right away. Have faith in the Father and in his timing. It isn't naive to say that his timing is perfect. It's the simple truth.

Remember that Satan will throw God's promises in your face at the most inauspicious times. He'll challenge your belief that God really does love you just when you're feeling you can't stand yourself. He'll try to sow seeds of doubt in your mind in order to undermine God's word to you. Don't let him. Practice the tenacious faith of Mary, of Elizabeth, of Jesus himself. If you do, you may indeed suffer for a time, but you will surely receive great blessings from a gracious God.

Father, sometimes it seems as though you're making a story out of my life that doesn't make sense. Things haven't turned out as I had imagined and hoped. I confess I'm disappointed. Still, I know that I haven't read the end of the story you're writing. You know what you're doing, Lord. Increase my faith and let the plot unfold.

NEVER DOUBT AN ANGEL

Then an angel of the Lord appeared to him [Zechariah], standing at the right side of the altar of incense. When Zechariah saw him, he was startled and was gripped with fear. But the angel said to him: "Do not be afraid, Zechariah; your prayer has been heard. Your wife Elizabeth will bear you a son, and you are to give him the name John."

Luke 1:11–13

The angel Gabriel must have been used to frightening people. In this case, he scared the wits out of John the Baptist's father. Zechariah and Elizabeth had been praying for years for a child, seemingly to no avail. Now, during Zechariah's priestly service in the temple, an angel appeared to him and stood near the altar of incense. In Scripture, incense symbolizes prayers ascending to heaven. The angel was standing near the altar on which the prayers of the Jewish people were offered to God. So it is fitting that Gabriel announced the answer to Zechariah's prayer in this way. For God had heard not only the prayers of this childless couple, but of all the Jews as well. The promised son would be a forerunner of the Messiah, the one who would liberate the Jews from their bondage.

Zechariah's reaction always amazes me. Even though he was terrified of the angel, he had the chutzpah to doubt the angelic message: "How do I know if you're telling the truth? Elizabeth and I are much too old to have children." The presence of an angel wasn't enough to convince this skeptic. He wanted proof positive.

Instead, he was punished for failing to believe Gabriel. The angel made him mute until the son he had promised would be born.

Have you ever prayed for something very difficult to believe in? In your heart, you doubt that God can or will do what you are asking. Even when God says yes, the doubt in our hearts often becomes apparent. Instead of erasing the last vestiges of unbelief, we cling to it, as Zechariah did.

God has already promised us many things in the Bible. He tells us that he loves us and that he forgives us, that there is no sin that Jesus cannot save us from. Think of the worst sin you can imagine. Chances are you read in the paper today about someone committing that sin: a woman who murdered her husband's lover, a minister who molested children, a dictator who slaughtered thousands of his own people, a serial murderer who preyed on women. Jesus died to save people like that. If that's true, why do we have such a hard time believing that God can forgive the kinds of habitual sins that many of us are guilty of: irritability, gossip, unkindness, cowardice, defensiveness, self-concern? We pray earnestly for forgiveness, yet we cling to our disbelief. God couldn't possibly forgive us. We set ourselves up as judges of what is and is not possible for God to do.

The encouraging thing about Zechariah's story is what he did with his tongue once his speech was restored after his son, John, was born. Rather than using it to challenge God's promise, he used it to praise him with this wonderful prophecy: "And you, child, will be called the prophet of the Most High; for you will go before the Lord to prepare his ways, to give knowledge of salvation to his people by the forgiveness of their sins. By the tender mercy of our God, the dawn from on high will break upon us" (Luke 1:76–78 NRSV).

Through the silent months, Zechariah's faith grew like a fruit to ripeness. And though the child he held in his arms was as yet only a seed of the promise, he no longer doubted the reliability of God's word. Instead, he proclaimed the message of God's mercy to any who would listen.

Lord, sometimes I wonder if I'm "believing impaired." I pray earnestly for something to happen but can't really believe that you will answer me favorably. Perhaps, like Zechariah, I'm so stubborn in my unbelief that even an angel would have difficulty convincing me. Father, forgive my intractable skepticism and open my soul to the risks of faith.

A SKY FULL OF ANGELS

There were shepherds living out in the fields nearby, keeping watch over their flocks at night. An angel of the Lord appeared to them, and the glory of the Lord shone around them, and they were terrified.

Luke 2:8–9

I magine the shepherds' astonishment to look up and see the night sky peppered with angels. Notice that the angels didn't announce the good news of Jesus' birth to any of the prominent people of Israel. They didn't appear to the mayor or the chief of police or even to King Herod in nearby Jerusalem, but to shepherds, plain men who stood guard over their noisy charges in the fields.

So often in Scripture, we see that God is not impressed with the things that impress us. He seems to go out of his way to drive this point home: his Son was born to an ordinary Jewish couple; Mary and Joseph were poor people; Jesus lived most of his life in obscurity. We are impressed that the King of the Universe was born in a stable. But think of the tremendous condescension that God had already displayed by planting the seed of divinity in the womb of a human being. The distance between God and his creatures is far greater than the distance between being born in a palace and being born in a stable.

The angels had a message to deliver, and they must have known that it would take root best in the soil of humility. So they told the shepherds about the Good Shepherd who would one day save them from their sins. And the shepherds believed.

The story of the shepherds convinces me that God is irresistibly attracted to humble hearts. It's as though the law of gravity has its spiritual equivalent. An object thrown from a high building will speed on until it hits the ground. So it is with God's grace as it courses from heaven to earth, coming to rest finally in the hearts of lowly men and women.

Father, have I become too sophisticated to hear your voice? Please keep me from pride in its many disguises and help me to learn from those who are humble of heart. Make my own heart a place of clarity, where your word can take root and bear fruit.

AN ANGEL AND A BIRTH ANNOUNCEMENT

A certain man of Zorah, named Manoah, from the clan of the Danites, had a wife who was sterile and remained childless. The angel of the LORD appeared to her and said, "You are sterile and childless, but you are going to conceive and have a son."

Judges 13:2–3

What is it with angels and birth announcements? We have already seen how the angel Gabriel announced the births of Jesus and of John the Baptist. A thousand years earlier, an angel appeared to the mother of Samson, the long-haired strongman, destined to save Israel from the might of the Philistines. In each case, God sent an angel to herald the coming birth of a special child. In each case, the circumstances were next to impossible. Either the woman was a virgin, barren, or well beyond childbearing age.

Often, the angels had the unenviable task of announcing the news to a skeptical parent-to-be. In Sarah's case, God himself told Abraham that his wife would bear a son. You can hardly blame the old man for falling down laughing at the news. It was like a headline out of *The National Enquirer*: "Baby boy born to a ninety-year-old woman!" What will they think of next?

God seemed to be making a point through these surprise announcements. He would fulfill his plan, in his way, in his good time. What was impossible for men and women was a simple matter for God. He would display his power by raising up deliverers for Israel from the wombs of barren women, or in one case from the womb of a virgin. He, the Lord, and he only, is the author of life.

Why did God go to such lengths, we wonder. Perhaps it was because he knew that fallen human beings would otherwise take the credit themselves. Unless the circumstances seemed impossibly bleak, his people would think they could handle life on their own. Their innate pride would not allow them to acknowledge their need for him and for his deliverance.

Sometimes God works in precisely this way in our own lives. The circumstances may look hopeless. We may have cried out to God for some need in our lives only to hear an echoing silence. Then, just when we are ready to abandon hope, God may bring something new to birth in our lives. The very thing we long for may be given us, not simply to benefit ourselves, but to bless others as well. We may sense that an angel is near to herald the news. When such things happen, we recognize that God is who he says he is—our deliverer, our shield, the author of life, the Lord who saves us.

God envisions the future in a way we cannot possibly comprehend. Like Samson's mother, like Sarah and Abraham, like Mary and Joseph, we can lift our prayers to God, confident that he hears us, knowing that he will answer us in his time and in his way. We may even chuckle a little, as Abraham did, when God makes us a promise that seems too good to be true.

> *Father, you know the prayer of my heart. You've heard it so many times, you must be tired of it. I know I'm asking you to do the impossible, but you've done it before, many times. Whatever you do, Lord, I will accept your answer. But if you choose to do the impossible, I'll make sure you receive all the credit.*

A Snow-White Angel

An angel of the Lord came down from heaven and, going to the tomb, rolled back the stone and sat on it. His appearance was like lightning, and his clothes were white as snow. The guards were so afraid of him that they shook and became like dead men. The angel said to the women, "Do not be afraid, for I know that you are looking for Jesus, who was crucified. He is not here; he has risen, just as he said."

Matthew 28:2–6

Mary Magdalene and another woman had come to the tomb to anoint the body of Jesus with spices, according to the custom of the Jews. Mary, you may remember, had been a woman from whom Jesus had cast out seven demons (Luke 8:2). She had gathered with a handful of Jesus' followers at his crucifixion, watching the one she loved, his body arched in torment, nailed hand and foot to a Roman cross. She stood as a witness in the darkness that had covered Jerusalem, a fitting pall for the shadows that filled her soul.

Mary had known in her own flesh the transforming power of Jesus' touch. She had little doubt of the hell from which he had saved her. Now he was in need and she could do nothing. She must have heard the chief priests and scribes as they shouted, "He saved others, but he cannot save himself! He's the King of Israel! Let him come down now from the cross, and we will believe in him" (Matthew 27:42). Their taunts would have pierced her soul. She was one of those he had saved. Now who was there to save him?

No one, apparently. The Messiah was dead. The hope of the Jewish people had disappeared in one bloody day. Now there was nothing left to do but to bury the dead. That's why she had come to the tomb. To do what needed to be done, no matter how deep her disappointment or how painful her grief. She followed Jesus when he had been alive. It seemed right to be near him in his death.

It must have been a wonderful assignment for the angel to proclaim the incredible good news to a woman whose heart was breaking. The guards posted at the tomb were terrified when they saw the angel, whose appearance was like lightening. They must have actually fallen over, because the Scripture says they "became like dead men."

Mary's disappointment and grief must have given way to bewilderment and then to joy. Jesus had overcome the death inside of her, and now he had himself come back to life.

Sometimes we feel that, like Mary, we are living between the crucifixion and the resurrection. We believe that Jesus rose from the dead, but we fail to experience resurrection joy because we are still waiting for God to heal some area of our life. Or perhaps we worry about someone we love, a spouse, parent, or child, who has not embraced a life of faith. We know that Jesus has acted with saving power in our own lives, but he does not seem to act with this same power in the lives of those closest to us.

At such times, it may help to reflect on the sorrow and disappointment of Mary Magdalene. She knew that Christ had the power to save her, but his power did not seem strong enough to save himself from crucifixion. Yet she stayed close to him, even in death. The angel said to her, "I know you are *looking* for Jesus who was crucified."

You may also be looking for Jesus, seeking a deeper assurance of his love and power. Keep looking and remember the angel's words, "Do not be afraid ... He is not here; he has risen, just as he said."

Jesus, what must it have been like to have seen your risen body, with the wounds still fresh upon your flesh? What kind of joy must Mary have felt when she finally encountered you in the garden, alive again? Lord, make Mary Magdalene's joy my own as I realize that nothing can separate me from you, "neither death nor life, neither angels nor demons, neither the present nor the future, nor any powers, neither height nor depth, nor anything else in all creation" (Romans 8:38–39).

5

Angels to the Rescue

Praise the LORD, you his angels,
you mighty ones who do his bidding,
who obey his word.
Praise the LORD, all his heavenly hosts,
you his servants who do his will.

Psalm 103:20–21

Far more effective than fire or police protection, angels have been known to perform the most daring rescue operations—walking around in a white-hot furnace, clamping shut the jaws of lions, blinding the eyes of prison guards. The angels seem to be up to any task God assigns.

This tells us something about the incredible power they possess. Angels are able to terrify their enemies, put tyrants to death, move swiftly from place to place, take a variety of shapes, and do what is generally unthinkable and impossible for us. They are creatures of another order. Knowing this, we can be very glad they are on our side.

The Bible is full of rescue stories. Many times we see angels coming to the aid of faithful men and women, who refuse to compromise with the spirit of the age. They care little whether they are out of sync with the times but only that they are in sync with God. Often they are willing to spend their lives for the sake of the truth.

People like Daniel, who risked a night with lions, impress us with their courage, as they should. But such people are not meant to be rare among believers. Around the world today, many Christians are paying the ultimate price of faith, surrendering both their freedom and their lives. All of us will face challenges, the temptation to make "little" compromises that promise to make life easier and more pleasant. Standing firm against such things will cost us something, perhaps even a great deal.

As we resist such pressures, we can be sure of God's protection. He may or may not rescue us from the difficulty we are in, but he will surely protect our souls from evil. The Father has multitudes of angels at his beck and call, and we can trust him to send them to our rescue at just the right moment. For the Lord "guards the lives of his faithful ones and delivers them from the hand of the wicked" (Psalm 97:10).

AN ANGEL SPEAKS
IN THE WILDERNESS

*God heard the boy crying, and the angel of God called to
Hagar from heaven and said to her, "What is the matter,
Hagar? Do not be afraid; God has heard the boy crying as he
lies there. Lift the boy up and take him by the hand, for I will
make him into a great nation." Then God opened her eyes
and she saw a well of water. She went and filled the skin with
water and gave the boy a drink.*

Genesis 21:17 – 19

Hagar was a single mother who was homeless, jobless, and
penniless. She had run out of food, out of water, and out
of hope. It seemed that she and her child would die alone in the
wilderness, with no one to mourn them.

You may recall that Hagar was the Egyptian slave of Sarah. As
Abraham's wife, Sarah had heard the incredible promise that God
would bless her and Abraham with a child, who would be the first
of countless descendants. Yet God's promise only made her laugh.
How could she possibly bear a son when she was already on the
wrong side of menopause?

Maybe God needed a little help to make this crazy promise
come true. Perhaps he meant to give them a son through her slave,
Hagar. So, with Sarah's blessing and encouragement, Abraham
slept with Hagar, and Hagar conceived a son, Ishmael.

Later, against all odds, Sarah gave birth to her own son, Isaac. Not surprisingly, a bitter rivalry grew up between the two women. Sarah insisted that Abraham toss Hagar and Ishmael out into the cold, and he did just that, offering the unhappy Hagar only some bread and a skin of water to help her and her child survive.

Since there wasn't any low-income housing in those days, Hagar was forced into the wilderness, where she wandered until her meager ration of bread and water ran out. On the point of despair, she sat down at some distance from her son, Ishmael. The last thing she wanted was to have to watch her only child suffer an agonizing death.

Hagar wept the tears of an abandoned and frightened woman, a stranger in a foreign land, with no one to notice her grief, or so she thought. Suddenly, in the midst of nowhere, an angel spoke to her from heaven. Hagar must have wondered if she had lost her mind after being so long without food and water. Yet the voice was real. The strong and comforting words of the angel dispelled her fear. A strange, new peace came with the angel's message. God had a plan and a purpose for her and her son. He would make Ishmael into a great nation! God would provide.

Notice that the angel didn't swoop down from heaven, carrying a glass of celestial water. Instead, he opened Hagar's eyes and showed her a well from which she could draw water. Abraham had given her a flask of water, which soon ran out. But God gave Hagar and Ishmael a well—water that would keep them alive and slake their thirst day after day.

Perhaps you are a parent, single or not, struggling to make a way for yourself and your children in the modern wilderness of this world. You may be able to feed and clothe your children, but you worry about their safety. Will they fall victim to the lure of sexual promiscuity, drugs, and violence? If you are single, you may feel lonely and in need of a partner to help you through life.

If so, ask God to open your eyes to his provision for you and your family, just as he did for Hagar. If God hadn't spoken to her through the angel, Hagar and her son would have died of thirst a stone's throw away from a well full of water. Perhaps God will send an angel to show you just how close his provision is for you.

Most of all, it helps to remember that God is the only one who can give you everything you need. You may think you simply need the right relationship, the right job, enough money. But in the last analysis, these things are but temporary provisions, just like the bread and flask of water that Abraham offered Hagar. All of us need to come to the living water, to the well that is Christ himself, in order to draw nourishment that will keep us going for the rest of our lives.

Father, the longer I live the more frightening life can seem. Friends and family haven't always come through when I've needed them. The things I thought I could count on have failed me. I'm beginning to realize that you are the only one I can always lean on. If you don't provide for me and for my children, who will? Lord, surely you know the plans you have for me—plans for my welfare and not for harm, to give me a future and a hope. When I call upon you, I know you will hear me.

"A Bonny White Man"

For he will command his angels concerning you
to guard you in all your ways.
On their hands they will bear you up,
so that you will not dash your foot against a stone.

Psalm 91:11–12 NRSV

One of the roles that angels play is to act as a kind of heavenly rescue squad. They often protect us from harm, both spiritual and physical. Sometimes these angelic rescues are obvious, but often they are not.

Samuel Rutherford was a seventeenth-century Christian who had an encounter with an angel. When Rutherford was a boy of five in Scotland, he fell into the village well. His frightened playmates ran to the nearest house for help.

Several men and women rushed to the rescue, fearful that the boy had already drowned. When they arrived, they were astonished to find the bedraggled Samuel, dripping wet and sitting on a mound of grass, not far from the well. "A bonny white man came and drew me out of the well," the boy told them. The well was far too deep for the boy to climb out of by himself. The "bonny white man" was an angel. That shining figure saw to it that Samuel would live out every one of the days that God had allotted him. Had God not intervened, Samuel Rutherford could not have achieved his purpose in life.

What was that purpose? Rutherford grew up to become a famous leader in the Church of Scotland. He played a prominent part in preparing *The Westminster Confession* and is credited with having written the *Shorter Catechism*. He also wrote *Lex Rex (Law Is King),* a book whose principles were picked up by the English philosopher John Locke. Locke incorporated these ideas into his own writing, and his fans included John Witherspoon, Thomas Jefferson, Benjamin Franklin, James Madison, and many other of America's founding fathers. These men extracted principles from Rutherford via Locke's writing that were to form the foundation of the new nation, principles like the three branches of government with each branch acting as a check and balance for the others.

"The bonny white man" had rescued a young boy, who would one day be used to play a strategic role in the church and in the founding of America.

Father, I know that you have created me for a special purpose that only I can fulfill. Thank you for preserving my life and guiding me along the way. Whenever I am in trouble, I will cry to you, to my God who fulfills his purpose for me.

ANGELS IN THE FIRE

Then Nebuchadnezzar said, "Praise be to the God of Shad-
rach, Meshach and Abednego, who has sent his angel and
rescued his servants! They trusted in him and defied the king's
command and were willing to give up their lives rather than
serve or worship any god except their own God."

Daniel 3:28

Nebuchadnezzar was the king of Babylon. Shadrach, Meshach, and Abednego were three young men from leading Jewish families who were made to serve in the king's palace after Jerusalem was captured by the powerful Babylonian army.

The problem began when the king erected a huge golden statue, six cubits by sixty cubits (as much as ten feet wide and a hundred feet tall). Nebuchadnezzar sent out word to all corners of the realm that his subjects were to worship the idol. The penalty for refusing was to be thrown into a blazing furnace, hot enough to incinerate even the coolest customer. So no one refused — no one, that is, but the three young Jewish men.

Nebuchadnezzar was enraged by their refusal and ordered the furnace to be heated to seven times its normal intensity. Shadrach, Meshach, and Abednego were bound and thrown into the furnace. It was so hot that the guards who threw the young men in were instantly consumed by the flames.

The king was astonished by what happened next. "Weren't there three men that we tied up and threw into the fire?" he exclaimed to his counselors. "Look! I see four men walking around in the fire, unbound and unhurt; and the fourth looks like a son of the gods."

Four men walking in the white-hot flames. Of course one was an angel so powerful that the king described him as a god. The three young men had no way of knowing they would miraculously survive their fiery ordeal. They couldn't be sure God would send an angel, but they trusted him for the outcome. They refused to dishonor him by bowing down to an idol, and God sent a fireproof angel to protect them as they walked freely in the furnace.

Notice that they were bound when they were cast into the furnace. But the king saw them walking around in the midst of the fire *unbound*. God had sent an angel not only to keep them from burning to death but to unfasten their bonds. In the midst of trial and persecution they were actually set free. Their story tells us that even in the most desperate circumstances, God can preserve our inner freedom as well as our lives.

No one is likely to command us to kneel before a golden statue today. Our culture promotes more subtle idols that demand our allegiance: sexual icons, success at any price, lust for power, unbridled materialism. The old idols keep popping up, disguised for modern times. Resisting the temptation to give into these cultural idols often entails great personal sacrifice.

Consider the single man or woman who refuses to give in to the fires of sexual passion, or the husband or wife who resists the temptation to sacrifice family life at the altar of career, or the unmarried woman who hears the dreaded news that she's pregnant but who resists the pressure to solve the "problem" with a quick visit to the local abortion clinic.

None of these is an easy choice to make. We will often suffer loss, fear, confusion, and pain in our quest to be faithful to what and whom we believe in. But as we trust God for the outcome, we will experience a new freedom. Perhaps an angel will even stand by our side in the midst of our distress, unbinding and protecting us from the devouring flames that threaten to consume us.

Lord, you know how hard it is for me to remain chaste when everything around me shouts the pleasures of intimacy with another person, regardless of whether I'm married to them. Sometimes, I'm tempted to think the price of following you is too high. Please give me the courage of these three young men to stand up for what is right no matter what it costs. Reassure me that as I do this you will make me a person who is truly free and full of joy.

THE ANGEL VERSUS
THE LIONS

When he [King Darius] came near the den, he called to Daniel in an anguished voice, "Daniel, servant of the living God, has your God, whom you serve continually, been able to rescue you from the lions?" Daniel answered, "O king, live forever! My God sent his angel, and he shut the mouths of the lions."

Daniel 6:20–22

King Darius was in a bind. He'd been tricked by officials in his kingdom who were jealous of Daniel's increasing influence over the king. They had persuaded Darius to sign a document proclaiming a thirty-day period in which it would be illegal to pray to anyone except the king. The penalty for ignoring the royal command would be a bloody death between the jaws of lions.

Daniel heard about the new law but continued to pray to God and praise him three times a day, just as he had always done. To make matters worse, he prayed boldly, in front of an open window, as was his habit. Clearly, Daniel was anything but a pragmatist. He could simply have stopped praying for a few days. What's a mere month in light of a lifetime of faithful prayer? Or at least he could have been a little more discreet. Why did he have to pray in front of a window, facing toward Jerusalem? However, Daniel refused to turn his back on his God in order to worship the powers of this world. He must have known that even small concessions would have encouraged a greater repression of faith. The initial edict lasted thirty days. What would stop the king from making the order permanent once he got everyone used to the idea?

Despite his regard for Daniel, the king had no choice but to abide by the decree he had issued and to cast Daniel into a den of ravenous lions. That done, Darius placed a stone over the den and sealed it with his own signet so that he would know if anyone moved the rock in an effort to rescue the hapless man.

After a restless night, the king returned the next morning and called out to Daniel to see whether, by some miracle, he was still alive. To the king's joy, Daniel replied that he was very much alive and that he had been preserved by an angel who had shut the lions' mouths.

Darius had rolled a stone over the lions' den, entombing Daniel with the raging beasts, and placing his signet on the stone. Yet an angel had pressed the lions' jaws shut and saved Daniel's life. Centuries later, religious authorities in Jerusalem would place a similar stone over the tomb of Jesus and seal it with a guard of soldiers to make sure no one would tamper with his grave. Once again, mere stones could not stop God's angels. For two angels appeared at the tomb of Jesus and addressed the women who came to anoint Jesus' body: "Why do you look for the living among the dead?" (Luke 24:5).

Both Daniel and Jesus refused to compromise their faith. God preserved the one from death and caused the other to conquer death once and for all. We may not face the kind of persecution that was meted out in the ancient world, but we will surely face pressures to compromise our beliefs in order to fit in with the world around us. When that happens, remember Daniel and Jesus. Remember that you can sell your soul by making the wrong kinds of compromises.

Remember that God protects the blameless man or woman. And last of all, remember the angels.

Jesus, I need your wisdom to know when to stand firm and when to compromise. Sometimes I pride myself too much on being able to stand in the middle. But you were controversial when you needed to be. Lord, you know I am not looking for trouble, but help me to stand firm when trouble comes my way. Don't let "being nice" be my highest goal. Give me the courage to be faithful, regardless of the consequences.

THE GREATEST RESCUE EVER

Then God said, "Take your son, your only son, Isaac, whom you love, and go to the region of Moriah. Sacrifice him there as a burnt offering on one of the mountains I will tell you about." ... Then he [Abraham] reached out his hand and took the knife to slay his son. But the angel of the LORD called out to him from heaven, "Abraham! Abraham!... Do not lay a hand on the boy." ... Abraham looked up and there in a thicket he saw a ram caught by its horns. He went over and took the ram and sacrificed it as a burnt offering instead of his son.

Genesis 22:2, 10–13

Something about this familiar story both deeply disturbs and strangely comforts us. How could a loving God ask Abraham to kill his own son, the son that he loved? Worse yet, how could God require Isaac's life as a sacrifice? We know from how the story ends that God was testing Abraham. Would he give back to God the one thing most valuable in his life, the son God had promised?

We can almost see the sweat dripping from the father's brow, gray-blue veins bulging across his temples, his powerful arm extended over the flesh of his son, knife in hand, ready to make the dreaded sacrifice.

The boy was bound to the rock like an animal ready for slaughter. What could possibly have been going through Isaac's mind in that moment? Did he catch and hold his father's gaze? What agony of love and terror must have passed from father to son and back again.

Then, when all hope had fled, an angel called out from heaven. "For God's sake, Abraham—don't harm the boy!" The pain that had passed between father and son turned to wonder. Abraham must have quickly untied Isaac, wrapping him in his arms, the man's tears mingling with the tears of the terrified boy. Isaac would live. Instead of a boy, a ram. A hapless animal caught in a thicket would provide the required sacrifice.

We breathe a sigh of relief as we read one of the most famous last-minute-rescue stories in biblical history. We marvel at the tremendous faith of Abraham. We doubt we could ever do what he did. We are disconcerted that God would even pretend to want a man to sacrifice his own son.

Yet the story of Abraham and Isaac points to the greatest rescue story of all time. Our confusion turns to awe and gratitude as we realize that what God did not require of Abraham, he required of himself. In Jesus, God's only Son, the Son the Father loved, we recognize the ultimate sacrifice. The "ram caught in the thicket" actually hinted at what was to be. The ram prefigured Jesus and his substitutionary death on Calvary. It might surprise you to learn that Jesus was nailed to a cross perhaps a quarter mile from Mount Moriah, possibly the very place where Abraham was prepared to sacrifice Isaac.

Centuries before Jesus even came on the scene, the Father was hinting at his plan, an incredibly daring and loving rescue operation. He knew how radical a remedy was needed to heal our brokenness and bring us back to him. When we are tempted to feel that God is asking too much of us, it may help to recall what he asked of himself. We understand and empathize with Abraham's anguish, but do we ever consider the terrible price the Father paid?

A moment's reflection will convince us that Jesus is the greatest gift of love the Father could have given us: "his Son, his only Son, whom he loved."

Father, I didn't realize the incredible price you paid when you gave your Son for me. I stand in awe of your mercy. Never let me doubt your love again or say that anything you ask is too hard to give. You gave me the One you loved the most; let me gladly surrender my soul and everything I am into your loving arms.

6

ANGELS IN DISGUISE

Art thou some god, some angel, or some devil?

William Shakespeare, *Julius Caesar*

With all this talk of angels, why isn't life more pleasant? The answer has to do with both the angels and with us. Life is often painful, confusing, and tragic because human beings have fallen from grace and turned their hearts from God. Bad as this is, that's not all there is to it.

Sometime before the dawn of history, God tested the faithfulness of his angels and found some of them wanting. Lucifer, or Satan, is thought to have been one of the most majestic of the angels, a powerful being who failed the test because of his enormous pride. Tradition holds that with him fell a third of the angels.

However many angels failed the test, we know that there are more than enough to go around. As such, they war for the souls of men and women, seeking to consign as many to destruction as possible. Martin Luther acknowledged this peril when he said, "The devil is also near and about us, incessantly tracking our steps, in order to deprive us of our lives, our saving health, and salvation." Luther also knew that God's power is more than sufficient to defeat every enemy.

It isn't pleasant to talk about the devil and it isn't wise to think about him too much, but we need to realize that not all the angels are on our side. The more we align ourselves with Christ in humility, faith, and obedience, the greater will be our safety and the stronger will be our confidence. The light will grow brighter and the darkness will diminish as God confirms his rule in our hearts.

An Insane Angel

～≈～

How you have fallen from heaven,
O morning star, son of the dawn!...
You said in your heart,
"I will ascend to heaven;
I will raise my throne
above the stars of God...
I will make myself like the Most High."
But you are brought down to the grave,
to the depths of the pit.

Isaiah 14:12 – 15

This passage probably refers to the fall of the King of Babylon. Yet many biblical scholars believe that it also refers to Satan's fall, before the beginning of human history.

Satan, or Lucifer (meaning "morning star" or "light bearer"), incited a rebellion in heaven. He wanted to take God's place, to sit on his throne and lord it over the universe. Eventually his pride forced him out of heaven.

Yet Satan's attempt to take over was nothing but an act of madness. How could a mere creature ever take the place of the Creator? To understand how ludicrous his position was, remember, for a moment, that we commit people who think they are God to insane asylums. Or imagine what would happen to me if I suddenly started telling everyone in sight that I was the emperor of Japan. Of course, this is a ridiculous scenario, but Satan's attempt to overthrow heaven was equally bizarre. As John Stott points out, "The essence of sin is man substituting himself for God, while the essence of salvation is God substituting himself for man." Satan's pride blinded him to the folly of his desire and evil took root in his heart.

Though the devil may be insane, he is powerfully insane, and, as such, he can tempt us to lose touch with reality too. This happens whenever we prefer our own will to God's. We do this in obvious ways: by committing murder, adultery, or grand larceny. But we also do it in more subtle ways. We want God to grant us a favor, to get us a particular job, a date, a raise in pay. Or we plead for him to heal someone instantaneously. Essentially, we want God to be our tool—to do our bidding whenever we command. All the while, Satan stands by to tell us that we are making reasonable demands.

What's wrong with asking for such things? you ask. Nothing at all. Jesus tells us that we should. But we begin to lose touch with reality whenever we try to force God to do what we want. We pile anxious prayers, one upon another. We attempt to persuade God to do whatever we ask by striving to behave perfectly, by following all the "rules." Sometimes we even use fasting (a helpful spiritual discipline, in itself) as a means of controlling God and getting him to do what we want. We fret and stew when we don't think God is acting as he should. We conclude that he doesn't love us enough to answer a few simple prayers.

Perhaps God loves us too much to do everything our way. He knows how miserable life would be if millions of "little gods" were ruling their respective universes. Often, God does answer our prayers in ways that delight us. But sometimes the answer is no. When that happens, let us take a moment to acknowledge his goodness, to thank him that he is in control and that we aren't. Let us pray that God will protect us from the long tentacles of pride, which try to strangle our reason and persuade us that we always know what's best. As we do this, a deeper humility and greater sanity will grow in us. Our minds will be freed from delusions large and small and we will grow in wisdom and peace.

Lord, you are God and I am but your creature who loves you. You know everything and I know only the merest trifles. You are all powerful and I am weak and vulnerable. You are everywhere and I can only be in one place at a time. You created me out of nothing and I can't make anything that lives. Your love fills the universe and my love is but a flame that flickers. Father, what a great combination we are, like a hand and a glove—you in your strength and me in my weakness!

A Telegram from Hell

To keep me from becoming conceited because of these surpass-ingly great revelations, there was given me a thorn in my flesh, a messenger of Satan, to torment me. Three times I pleaded with the Lord to take it away from me. But he said to me, "My grace is sufficient for you, for my power is made perfect in weakness."

2 Corinthians 12:7–9

We have seen that one of the roles angels play in human affairs is to convey messages between God and human beings. Unfortunately, it seems that Satan likes to send messages of his own from time to time.

In the apostle Paul's case, we don't know what his "thorn in the flesh" was, his "messenger from Satan." All we know is that it came to him after he had a remarkable vision in which he was caught up into heaven itself. We know from what Paul says that God allowed the enemy to act as the messenger. Two verses later, Paul tells the Corinthians that "for Christ's sake I delight in weaknesses, in insults, in hardships, in persecutions, in difficulties. For when I am weak, then I am strong" (2 Corinthians 12:10). Any of these things could describe the "thorn" that Paul mentioned. Perhaps he left it deliber-ately vague so that you and I might realize that we too will have our own "thorns," though our circumstances may differ from his.

You can be sure that Paul wasn't happy to receive this black telegram from Satan. So he pleaded with God, not once, but three times. "Please, Lord, take it away. It's from Satan. How can it possibly be good for me?" Paul didn't respond to his affliction by simply resigning himself to his fate. He took the problem straight to God, and God gave Paul an answer—not the one he wanted but the one he accepted. Satan had a message for Paul, but God had a deeper message. Whatever Paul suffered would provide a tremendous opportunity for him to actually become more powerful in Christ. In God's strange economy, power was perfected in weakness. His grace would cause Paul to be strengthened if only Paul would endure his trial patiently.

Perhaps you have received a few messages from Satan too, messages that frighten or discourage you or make you doubt God's love. The messages that come from below can arrive in a variety of ways: a tongue-lashing from your boss, a crippling disease, a catastrophe that strikes your family. The possibilities are endless. Perhaps God has permitted you or someone you love to suffer deeply. Plead to God to take your affliction away. Don't accept the lie that you deserve whatever bad things happen. But listen while you're in God's presence, pleading your case. For he might have a deeper message than the one Satan intends to deliver. God might have a secret he can share with you in no other way. Perhaps he will whisper a word that will help you make sense out of life and give you greater hope and confidence for the future.

Father, sometimes I am so confused about my life. Something difficult happens and I wonder if you're punishing me. I become fearful, tense, and confused. But then I remember who the "author of confusion" really is—my enemy and yours. Lord, I ask you to protect me and help me to pierce through this present darkness to understand what's really going on.

A CASE OF POSSESSION

They sailed to the region of the Gerasenes, which is across the lake from Galilee. When Jesus stepped ashore, he was met by a demon-possessed man from the town. For a long time this man had not worn clothes or lived in a house, but had lived in the tombs.

Luke 8:26–27

How would you like it if the first person who greeted you in a strange city was a dangerous lunatic? That's exactly who met Jesus and his disciples when they crossed the Sea of Galilee and stepped out on shore. The local people had tried to bind the man in chains, but with demonic strength he would merely break the shackles and escape to roam among the tombs. The picture Luke paints is worse than anything out of an old Bela Lugosi film.

Confronted by such a person, most of us would have rushed back to the boat and shoved off as quickly as possible. But Jesus had crossed Galilee in a storm, precisely to heal this man, and he would not turn back. We are frightened and repulsed. Jesus is touched with compassion for a soul in torment.

Instead of rushing upon them in a fury, the demonized man falls down at Jesus' feet and shouts at the top of his voice, "What do you want with me, Jesus, Son of the Most High God? I beg you, don't torture me." The demons were speaking, not the man. The greater power and authority of Jesus forced them to fall at his feet, imploring his mercy. But Jesus had mercy on the man, not on the demons. He commanded them to come out and the man was restored to his right mind.

As modern men and women, we sometimes have difficulty with such stories. Didn't these people mistake mental illness with demonic possession? Such mistakes were undoubtedly made in ancient Israel, but Jesus knew precisely what he was dealing with.

Jesus was not afraid of the powers of darkness that inhabited this man. He knew his own power was far greater. And so he used it to lovingly restore the man. Jesus' desire to heal our afflictions, whether emotionally, physically, or spiritually based, is the same today.

God's ultimate hope for every one of us is that we will enjoy an intimate and loving relationship with him. Our communion with him is characterized by love, freedom, joy, and respect. The fallen angels, however, seek an unholy and counterfeit communion, one characterized by hatred, domination, enslavement, and terror. Often evil is merely a counterfeit of the good.

We are naive if we fail to believe that powerful forces of evil are at work in the world today. But we make an even greater mistake if we fail to understand that God's power is far greater than Satan's. Two thousand years ago, Jesus commanded the unclean spirits to leave. He does the same today.

Jesus, if I am to know fear in my life, may it be the fear of God that rules me. Never let me fall into the hands of my enemy, but keep me safe within your powerful and protective arms. Don't let me be frightened or repulsed by the suffering of others, but touch my heart with compassion so that I might, in turn, touch others with your love.

New Age Angels

For Satan himself masquerades as an angel of light.

2 Corinthians 11:14

I grew up in an era that was embarrassed by religion. Personal religious beliefs were never a subject of polite conversation. Whatever could not be seen or touched simply did not really exist. To suggest otherwise marked you as either a fool or a charlatan.

Ironically, this sophisticated skepticism has actually increased our susceptibility to all kinds of primitive beliefs and superstitions. Like a beach ball pushed under water only to pop up a few feet away, our spiritual nature and spiritual longings eventually reassert themselves, sometimes in strange ways. Not surprisingly, our culture is now awash with every variety of superstition, including belief in ghosts, witches, reincarnation, spirit guides, and shamanism.

Spiritual hunger is good in one sense but dangerous in another. It is like setting someone loose in a supermarket when they haven't eaten for three days. They may bring home every kind of food imaginable, some of which begins to smell bad and taste worse after a few days on the shelf.

This new appetite is evident in the New Age movement, where a smorgasbord of spirituality is presented from which devotees can choose what they like and discard what they don't.

In spiritual matters, we need wise guides. We need to cultivate discernment so that we can tell what is from God and what is not. If we are seeking spiritual thrills or power rather than the truth, we can endanger our souls by dabbling in the supernatural. Scripture calls Satan the "father of lies." He's the slickest con man of all time, and one of his favorite ploys is to dress up as an angel of light. If you fall for the disguise and open yourself to such a being, you may never know what hit you.

Author Geddes MacGregor reinforces this point when he says, "The most terrible of the afflictions that attend him who loses purity of heart is that he loses with it the power to detect evil intent when it approaches him as a wolf attired in the benign clothing of a sheep. He is an easy prey: a sitting duck for the devil. He has lost the clarity of moral vision that penetrates every disguise and sees through to the spiritual reality behind it."

As Christians, we are guided by the Holy Spirit and by God's Word in the Bible. No matter how dazzling the vision, we must test the spirits against the Word of God and not allow our spiritual hungers to confuse our judgment. If we do, we will be able to spot a fake whenever we see it. Far from being a sitting duck for the devil, we will have the wisdom to discern the spirits, no matter how ingeniously disguised.

Lord, I know that you will keep me on the right path if it's really you I'm seeking. Help me not to search for the sensational, but to seek true holiness. You know that the search is neither glamorous nor easy. You said yourself that the road was narrow and hard. Help me, Lord, to follow you along that road and not to veer onto other paths, no matter how attractive they may seem.

TEMPTED IN EDEN

＜Ӡ＞

Now the serpent was more crafty than any of the wild animals the LORD God had made. He said to the woman, "Did God really say, 'You must not eat from any tree in the garden'?"

Genesis 3:1

Adam and Eve had it made. They had each other. They lived in Paradise. And they enjoyed perfect intimacy with their Creator. Then they spoiled everything. They listened to the voice of the tempter, who placed a seed of doubt in Eve's mind.

We all know the old story. Today we suffer the painful consequences. When my niece Jenny was only five years old, she said something that startled me. We were driving along a city street in the middle of winter when we passed a graveyard. Jenny knew that cemeteries were filled with the bones of dead people. She turned to me and sighed, "I wish Adam and Eve had never sinned." Her little face was so sad, her voice so full of sorrow that it nearly broke my heart. Despite her tender years, she had already experienced enough pain to comprehend the dilemma of our race.

Genesis says that Adam and Eve tried to hide from God when he called their names in the garden. They knew something was terribly wrong. In fact, sin had ripped a hole in their hearts large enough to swallow the universe. No longer would they converse with God in the garden in the cool of the day. No longer would they enjoy one another's company without accusation forming a barrier between them. No longer would they even understand their own motivations. They had become alienated from God, from each other, and from themselves. All was agony, loss, and endless confusion.

God expelled them from the garden of his presence but then promised them a Savior. Unlike the angels, human beings would be granted another chance. Somewhere in the long centuries ahead, a child would be born who would crush the head of the serpent. Jesus is the One who fulfills the promise. He is a beacon in the dark night of sin. He is the sinless one who by his obedience reverses our disobedience. Because Jesus obeyed his Father to the end, you and I have another chance. Because of him we have the power to prefer God's will to ours. We have the grace to believe that God is telling the truth after all. What can we say to such mercy? We can reply most eloquently with our obedience. It is the best gift of love we could ever give the Father.

In Adam and Eve the world made a bad beginning. But in Christ, the world begins anew. He is the firstborn of the new creation, and we are the ones who follow in his steps.

Father, please forgive my foolishness. So many times I have preferred my version of what is good for me to yours. Sometimes I have even considered your laws arbitrary and unnecessary. I, too, have been deceived by the serpent. Let love for you compel me as it did Jesus. Never let me be mastered by the glamour of evil, but purify my heart so that I might one day be restored to Paradise.

7

Angels and the Unseen War

❧

*The wars among nations on earth are merely popgun affairs
compared to the fierceness of battle in the spiritual unseen world.*

Billy Graham

Michael the archangel is depicted in Scripture as a great warrior, leading the host of heaven against all the demons of hell. He is also thought to be the guardian protector of God's people. It is comforting to know that powerful angels like Michael are engaged in the battle alongside us.

Though the fight is real, sometimes we wage it in anything but a wise manner. Immature Christians particularly can become so excited about talk of weapons and warfare that they think spiritual combat involves shouting commands against the enemy and singing warlike songs. The truth is that spiritual warfare is only one part of the Christian life—and not a very glamorous part at that. If we insist on waging it in the flesh, we will have nothing but spiritual bruises to show for it.

We need to realize that God allows us to engage in the battle in order to strengthen us. As we resist the enticements of evil, we grow in maturity. The longer we live in obedience to Christ, the greater will be our ability to destroy the strongholds of the enemy. Our weapons may impress no one, but they will be effective enough to win the war: holiness, faith, meekness, long-suffering, truth, and the knowledge of God's Word.

We do need zeal for the struggle, but let's make certain it's a godly zeal rather than some fleshly version that will only get us into trouble. Most of all, let's remember that it's Christ who leads us into battle and who keeps us safe. Without him, we wouldn't have a chance. With him, we have the victory.

WHEN THE DEVIL LIVES NEXT DOOR

And there was war in heaven. Michael and his angels fought against the dragon, and the dragon and his angels fought back. But he was not strong enough, and they lost their place in heaven. The great dragon was hurled down—that ancient serpent called the devil, or Satan, who leads the whole world astray. He was hurled to the earth, and his angels with him.

Revelation 12:7–9

Like it or not, real estate values suffer whenever "undesirable elements" move into a neighborhood. Imagine how the real estate we call "earth" suffered when Satan got kicked out of heaven and thrown down to earth. I don't know about you, but I have been tempted to utter a sarcastic "thanks a lot" to Michael and his angels for ejecting Satan and his cohorts from the heavenly realms. Couldn't they have tossed him into an unpopulated region of the universe? In a sense, the devil is now everyone's neighbor. And he is definitely spoiling the neighborhood.

At least we can be thankful that Scripture warns us that the war that began in heaven now rages on earth, sometimes in our own backyard. In fact, the book of Revelation says that the evil one makes war on "those who keep the commandments of God and hold the testimony of Jesus" (Revelation 12:17), After all, it's better to know you're in a war and to arm yourself accordingly than to wander around, innocently stepping on land mines.

But let's get back to the neighborhood. What would you do if criminals started moving in? You could sell your house, but what if criminal elements have moved in everywhere? If even the best neighborhoods had a crook on every corner? You would simply be trading one bad neighborhood for another.

The best thing you could do in such a situation would be to arm and equip yourself. You would, no doubt, install greater security measures in your home, and you might even purchase weapons and take a course in self-defense. You would also appeal to the authorities for help.

Knowing that the devil is on the loose is a sobering matter. But the Scriptures tell us how to engage in spiritual combat so that we needn't be afraid of Satan, for "the one who is in you [Jesus] is greater than the one who is in the world" (1 John 4:4). We need to arm ourselves with the tactics and weapons of heaven rather than the strategies of this world. The more the gospel penetrates our lives, the more we will perceive that the weapons of Christ are humility, obedience to the Father, trust and faith, truth, right living, and the Word of God, which is the "sword of the Spirit" (Ephesians 6:17). As we appeal to God's authority for dealing with the attacks of our enemy, we will grow in confidence that Christ has given his followers authority over the evil one.

We are not to let the neighborhood go to the devil, but we are to claim this earth for God's kingdom. As Scripture says, "The earth is the LORD's, and everything in it" (Psalm 24:1). Jesus is in the business of recapturing territory for God, and we are enlisted in his army. That's why Satan so frequently takes aim at Christians. As we fight the enemy, let us remember the prayer that Jesus taught us: "Our Father, which art in heaven, Hallowed be thy name. Thy kingdom come, Thy will be done, in earth, as it is in heaven" (Matthew 6:9 – 10 KJV). Let's bring the kingdom into our own neighborhoods. The more that heaven encroaches upon the earth, the less our enemy will like it here.

Father, help me not to be naive about the spiritual conflict that rages about me. Worse yet, don't let me try to stand in my own strength. Instead, clothe me with integrity, with faith in you, with obedience to your commandments, with the knowledge of what your Son has done for me, and with the tremendous power of your Word. That way I will be strong in the strength of your power.

THE PRINCE
OF THIS WORLD

You were dead through the trespasses and sins in which you once lived, following the course of this world, following the ruler of the power of the air, the spirit that is now at work among those who are disobedient.

Ephesians 2:1–2 NRSV

J. R. R. Tolkien wrote an enormously popular fantasy trilogy entitled *The Lord of the Rings*. The main character, Frodo Baggins, possessed a ring of great power. Among other things, the ring had the power to render its wearer invisible to most eyes. Frodo's perilous quest involved traveling to Mount Doom in the land of Mordor in order to consign the ring to the flames of the mountain, thus destroying its terrible power forever.

Frodo and his companions were pursued by black riders, who sought to murder them and take the ring. In one encounter, Frodo panicked and slipped the ring on his finger in the hopes that it would hide him from his pursuers. What he failed to realize was that the ring actually made him visible to the evil riders and invisible to his companions. He was nearly killed in the ensuing fray. Each time Frodo succumbed to temptation by wearing the ring, he became more vulnerable to its powerful enchantments.

Disobedience works much like Frodo's ring. In our hearts, we know what God requires of us. But our pride, our fears, and our desires tempt us to obey our will rather than God's. We prefer our definition of what is good for us to God's definition.

In his letter to the Ephesians, Paul makes it clear that whoever lives a life of disobedience to God has the ruler of the power of the air, or Satan, at work in them. The prince of this world actually feeds on our disobedience. Living a life of disobedience is like putting Frodo's ring on your finger. It makes you vulnerable to all kinds of evil. A habit of disobedience puts you firmly in the power of Satan.

Loving God, by contrast, involves much more than simply paying lip service to him. It requires a total surrender of your life into the hands of God, obeying his commands whether or not you feel like it. As you grow in a life of obedience, your power to resist evil will increase. Much like aerobic exercise that increases lung capacity, preferring God's will to your own can increase your spiritual stamina. Rather than having the prince of this world at work in your life, you will have the power of Jesus at work within. You will be stronger and more joyful, better able to resist the enticements of the evil angels, no matter how appealing they may seem.

Jesus, you once said that your food was to do the will of your Father in heaven. I pray that this will be my food also. Nourish me by the power of your Holy Spirit that I may form a habit of obedience that will delight your angels and put my enemy to flight.

THE BREAD OF ANGELS

But he himself [Elijah] went a day's journey into the wilderness.... He asked that he might die: "It is enough; now, O LORD, take away my life."... Suddenly an angel touched him and said to him, "Get up and eat."... He got up, and ate and drank; then he went in the strength of that food forty days and forty nights to Horeb the mount of God.

1 Kings 19:4–5, 8 NRSV

Elijah was an Old Testament prophet who spoke the word of the Lord in an age of idolatry. He had just enjoyed a spectacular victory over false prophets, who were destroyed after Elijah called down fire from heaven and won a contest with them. Now we see him on the run, afraid of the evil queen Jezebel, whose prophets he had slain. Elijah was so fearful and depressed that he asked God to take his life. But God had a better idea.

Instead, he sent an angel to touch him and nourish him in the wilderness. The food the angel brought was enough to keep Elijah going for the next forty days and nights. That's what you call high-energy snacking!

Not many of us will ever find ourselves on the lam, fleeing an evil queen. Neither are we likely to call down fire from heaven. But each of us is called to witness to the living God, and sometimes our witness will not be appreciated. Whenever we work against the idols of the age—against the lust for money, power, and sex—we will encounter great spiritual opposition.

Notice that Elijah should have been elated rather than depressed. He has just won the greatest spiritual victory of his lifetime. God had shown his power in a very dramatic way. Yet he is afraid and dejected. The tremendous faith he displayed when surrounded by the false prophets had given way to exhaustion and doubt. So much so that he does not want to go on living. Despite God's miraculous display of power on Mount Carmel, Jezebel had not bet been overthrown.

Elijah's experience is sometimes our own. We may have seen God work through us or through our prayers in a powerful new way. And yet we experience fear and dejection when we face an apparent setback. If so, we may be the target, as Elijah was, of a spiritual counterattack. We have just encroached on enemy territory, and he is not happy.

Yet God did not leave Elijah to deal with his depression on his own. Instead, he sent one of his faithful angels to touch his servant and feed him the bread of heaven. You may recall that Jesus once told his disciples that he had food to eat that they did not know about. His food was to do the will of his Father in heaven. As we seek to do God's will, to be his witnesses to an unbelieving world, we too will be nourished by the bread of angels, and our exhaustion and depression will give way to faith and hope in the incredible provision of our God.

Father, sometimes I get so tired of the fight that I wonder if it's really worth it. I even start to wonder if I've gained any ground at all. At such times, help me to see the true state of things. Don't let my enemy discourage me with lies about his power. Instead, feed me with the bread of angels and give me joy in the midst of the battle.

FIGHTING ON THE SIDE
OF THE ANGELS

Our struggle is not against flesh and blood, but against the rulers, against the authorities, against the powers of this dark world and against the spiritual forces of evil in the heavenly realms.

Ephesians 6:12

Paul is not committing the sin of hyperbole when he says that our struggles are against the cosmic powers of darkness. The Bible is nothing if not a record of the conflict between good and evil.

But we are so easily fooled into thinking that mere human beings are our primary enemies. On the religious front, Christians scandalize the world by squabbling and name-calling among themselves. Catholics and Protestants view each other with predictable suspicion. And purists take potshots at anyone who doesn't measure up to their version of Christianity.

Of course it's important to fight for the solid meat of the gospel, for the truths of our faith. But we are often divided on the peripherals, matters that are not central to what C. S. Lewis calls "mere Christianity." No denomination or group is innocent in this regard. You name it, and we can find something to fight about. In the meantime, men and women perish for failure to hear the gospel.

This same kind of contentiousness often characterizes our dealings on the political front. We fall victim to what has been called the political illusion: we begin to believe that every problem we face has a political solution. This adds a new intensity to the political arena, where we come just short of calling our opponent the antichrist. The truth is, we sometimes conduct ourselves in the political realm as anything but men and women whose conduct is shaped by the kindness of Christ.

True, religious and political differences can be tremendously important. But sometimes, the evil one throws them in our faces as a smokescreen, obscuring what is really going on. For instance, we may be ruled by corrupt politicians and judges because we are simply getting what we have asked for as a nation. God may be allowing us to experience the fruit of our rebellion against him. Repentance may change things in a way that political campaigning cannot. We must develop both a spiritual and a political outlook. If we don't look below the surface to see what is going on spiritually, we will often miss the point.

Scripture tells us we are in a battle, but how sad if we mistake the real enemy and begin to fight each other instead. Our enemies are not mere flesh and blood. We fight spiritual powers, and we must fight them with spiritual weapons. While Satan and his angels employ the weapons of hatred—deceit, slander, fear, greed, and confusion—we are called to employ the weapons of love—forgiveness, mercy, faith, truth, discernment, prayer, sacrifice, and righteousness. The battle is real. We cannot ignore it. But neither can we enter the fray with delusions about who the enemy is and how we are to fight. If we want to fight on the side of the angels, we need to heed Paul's warning.

Father, help me to be wise as a serpent and innocent as a dove. Help me to know who my real enemy is and how I am to fight. Confirm me in self-control so that I won't give in to the temptation to use dirty tricks and name-calling in the cause of "righteousness." Let me instead use the weapons of prayer, perseverance, patience, truth, obedience, and love.

ANGELS PROTECT US
FROM EVIL

As Pharaoh drew near, the Israelites looked back, and there were the Egyptians advancing on them.... The angel of God who was going before the Israelite army moved and went behind them; and the pillar of cloud moved from in front of them and took its place behind them. It came between the army of Egypt and the army of Israel. And so the cloud was there with the darkness, and it lit up the night; one did not come near the other all night.

Exodus 14:10, 19–20 NRSV

Anyone over forty probably can't help but picture the Israelite march to the Red Sea like this: a long-haired Charlton Heston with staff in hand extended over the water, while an evil-looking Yul Brynner thunders on in hot pursuit. The Red Sea in the movie *The Ten Commandments*, we later discovered, was made of Jello. Thank you, Cecil B. DeMille! But the real Exodus had far more impressive special effects.

The Israelites escaped enslavement by marvelous acts of God—horrific plagues rained from heaven upon their Egyptian oppressors. But Pharaoh's hard heart could not stand the thought of Moses leading the Jewish people to freedom. So he pursued them in the desert, threatening to overtake them as they approached the Red Sea. It would be so easy for him. His powerful army would swiftly crush the raggedy band of slaves. But Pharaoh, stubborn and stupid in his wickedness, forgot about the angels.

The angel and the pillar of cloud, a symbol of God's presence, moved from the front of the people to take up protective positions behind them. As we know, Pharaoh was not able to catch the Israelites, who passed through the waters in safety. Still he stubbornly pursued them, but the walls of water engulfed him and his army, suffocating them in its turbulent wake.

The story of the exodus is played out in miniature in the life of every believer. Like the Jews of old, we are held in bondage. Pharaoh represents Satan, who enslaves every person who does not belong to God. But God saves us from our enemy and leads us into freedom and into the promised land of his presence.

While we live on earth, we are involved in this exodus journey. Often, our pilgrimage seems agonizingly slow and confusing. We seem to wander in a desert of our own weakness and sin. Our faith is tested by difficulty. We have fears, many of which are real. It is not only "the things that go bump in the night" that terrify us.

But like the Jewish people fleeing the wrath of Pharaoh, we can be certain that God will surround us with his protection. He will send angels to battle our enemy and a pillar of fire to brighten our darkness. Though evil may threaten, it will never overwhelm us. We can take comfort from the prayer attributed to Patrick of Ireland: "Christ be with me, Christ before me, Christ after me, Christ within me, Christ beneath me, Christ above me, Christ at my right hand, Christ at my left." Surrounded by Christ, we will pass safely through this world to the next.

Lord, you know the spiritual dangers I have already passed through. It was your hand that kept me safe over and over again. Help me to fear neither the desert nor the darkness, but to take each step knowing that I am closer to the day when I will see you face to face, when I will live in your presence forever.

8

EARTHLY ANGELS

*The golden moments in the stream of life rush past us
and we see nothing but sand; the angels come to visit us,
and we only know them when they are gone.*

George Eliot

All God's angels come to us disguised.

James Russell Lowell

Though we may never have had an angelic encounter of a supernatural kind, most of us have had more than a few experiences with what some have called earthly angels — human beings who have touched us in some deep and surprising way when we needed help.

I remember a classmate who comforted me when my sister died suddenly in an automobile accident. Sue was sixteen when she was killed, and I was so stunned by her death that I was unable to express my grief to anyone, even to my family. Though the two of us had sometimes argued, as sisters do, we had always been close. We shared the same room and even the same bed. I remember the imaginary line that separated her side from mine and the protests that erupted whenever either of us breached that border.

In the aftermath of her death, the pain felt too sharp to share, the memory of her too sacred to speak of. How could anyone understand that I would have given anything just to hear her accusing me one more time of "breathing" onto her side of the bed? But now when I lay down to sleep there was only emptiness and silence.

Not long after the accident a girl in my class befriended me, speaking about her grief for a brother who had died the year before. She must have sensed my own need for someone to confide in. Looking back, I can see how God used my friend Mary to help me get through that time and begin the healing process.

Earthly angels like my friend come in all colors, sizes, and shapes. Though not angelic beings, they still act as divine messengers, people who reveal something important about God's personal love and care for us. In the stories that follow, let God remind you of times in your life when he has brought you help in human form — a friend to come alongside at just the right moment. Thank him for showing his love to you through other human beings.

While you're at it, why not volunteer to become an "angel" yourself. You need only ask God to guide you to others in need. Remember, too, that he has already given you the one human being who will never let you down. Praise him for the greatest gift of all, his only Son, Jesus, who is the perfect expression of his love.

AN EARTHLY ANGEL
AND A HEALING DREAM

❦

Precious in the sight of the LORD is the death of his saints.
Psalm 116:15

Charlene Ann Baumbich got a phone call that her mother had suffered a massive stroke. Two weeks later, her mother was dead. Here is the story of her encounter with an earthly angel and of a powerful dream that healed her memory of her mother's last days:

"My mother had been named after a racehorse. Though I never met the horse, I always knew this mother of mine was a champion in her own right—beautiful, graceful, fast-paced, and vibrant. As far as I know, Nellie Ruth hadn't an enemy in the world, even though she once emptied a punch bowl over the head of a blonde bombshell who was putting the moves on my dad.

"When Mom was nine months pregnant, she drove a delivery truck to help my father's new business stay afloat. Both feminine and fearless, she could shoot skeet or skin a rabbit with the best of them. Once she even shot a fox that made its way into the basement of our farm. She had energy, passion, and guts. A person of unstoppable spunk, she was beautiful both inside and out.

"Mom never went anywhere without her toenails painted, her hair done, and perfume trailing. Never, until the night of January 14, 1975. She was only fifty-six years old when she suffered a massive stroke. I got the call in the middle of the night and flew to Albuquerque the next morning, fearing the worst.

"My fear exploded the moment I walked into her hospital room. Surely that body lying on the bed couldn't belong to my mother! All the life, the beauty, the laughter had fled. There was only a limp figure, hooked to a machine, with tubes protruding from every orifice. It was more than I could bear.

"For the next ten days I stayed with Mom, combing her hair, misting her body with cologne, clasping her hand, desperately hoping to restore some semblance of the woman I had known and loved. I tried not to cry in her presence, unsure whether she could sense my tears. Her neurologist pressured us to pull the plug, but we just couldn't. We had hardly adjusted to the idea of her illness when he told us that her condition was hopeless: 'It's as though someone extracted your mother's brains, scrambled them, and stuffed them back into her head. They're useless,' he explained in the most brutal bedside manner you can imagine. We didn't know whether Mother would die or whether she would live another thirty years in that horrible condition.

"In the midst of this, I met an angel named Dorothy Booker. To pass the time, I had been working on a macramé project, when this wonderful, round, black woman, whose mother was also in the hospital, started talking to me. Before I knew it, I began pouring out my grief and pain. So many decisions needed to be made about Mom's care. I didn't know what to do. I had never lived through a crisis without drawing strength from her, and now she was my crisis.

"Mom was the one who always told me how beautiful I was. She lavished praise on my cleverness. She admired every hokey crochet project as though it were the most exquisite work of art. She was the foundation I stood on, the ground that steadied me. If she wasn't there to tell me these things, who would be? What would I do without her bountiful laughter?

"Dorothy Booker enfolded me in her comforting bosom as I sobbed out my grief. 'Child, the Lord has your mamma right here in the palm of his hand. No matter what you decide, he knows what's best for your mamma. He loves your mamma more than you can imagine, and he is in charge of your mamma.' Dorothy eased my grief and comforted me like the angel she was.

"After ten days, I returned to my family in the Midwest. Sadly, my last vision of my mother was a tragic one. Colorless, an oxygen mask covered her mouth, and she lay with one eye open and the other closed. What a horrible last impression of my smiling, joyous, large-hearted mother! The memory haunted me.

"Four days later I got the news that Mom had died. Somehow I made it through the funeral, though I was falling apart inside. Weeks followed in which I found myself irritated at anyone who crossed my path. I couldn't understand how friends and family had suddenly grown so stupid! No matter what they did, they drove me to distraction. I began to realize I was the one with the problem.

"Then I had a dream more vivid and real than any I have ever experienced. I saw my mother standing in a glass telephone booth filled with light. The background was smoky gray and misty, somewhat ethereal. But a bright light surrounded my mother. I couldn't talk to her or touch her, and she didn't talk to me. But we communicated. Her face was absolutely at peace, and she was smiling at me with a brilliance I had never seen before. I can only say she looked beatific. Healed, whole, and utterly happy. It was as though she were saying, 'Charlene, I'm well and you are going to be all right. You need to know this.'

"I woke up weeping but completely at peace. It was an absolute gift of God. The dream had diminished the ugly memories of my mother's illness and replaced them with the most beautiful vision of her I have ever seen. Dorothy Booker's words came back to me. 'Child, the Lord has your mamma right here in the palm of his hand.' My mother was well, and so was I in that moment.

"So many people are burdened by tragic memories of a loved one's death. I hope the story of my dream will help diminish such memories for others, so that they will not remember their loved ones in a way that utterly contradicts who they were in life. Despite my mother's suffering, I know she is more beautiful than ever. When I close my eyes, I can see her laughing up a storm, enjoying herself as never before. Knowing she is well and with God gives me joy."

Lord, you are a refuge for us. Underneath are your ever-loving, everlasting arms.

THREE ANGELS
TO THE RESCUE

When you walk through the fire,
   you will not be burned;
   the flames will not set you ablaze.
For I am the LORD, your God,
   the Holy One of Israel, your Savior.

Isaiah 43:2–3

Roseanne Koskie didn't have a clue that November 10, 1993, would be different than any other day. If she had, she might have chosen to stay in bed that morning.

"I drive a '91 Plymouth Acclaim," she explained. "It never gave me any trouble until the day a coworker and I decided to have lunch at Grandy's, a restaurant on the east side of El Paso. Over lunch we discussed business and then prepared to leave. But there was only one problem. My car wouldn't start.

"I tried the ignition again, but nothing happened; the engine wouldn't turn over. My friend, Sandy, suggested I give it some gas, but I explained that this was a fuel-injected engine. I didn't need to press the accelerator for the cylinders to fire. But try as I might, the car wouldn't start. Since we were parked on an incline, we began to wonder if somehow fuel wasn't getting through the line. Perhaps it needed a little extra oomph to get things moving. So I pumped the pedal a couple of times. But still, nothing happened. At that point, Sandy offered to go back into the restaurant to call for help.

"I sat in the car for a minute, when suddenly, I noticed what looked like flames flicking from under the hood. It couldn't be fire, I thought. The engine never even started. Without thinking, I got out of the car and raised the hood. Sure enough, the front of the car was on fire. I ran to the trunk for a blanket to smother the flames, but as I raced back to the front of the car, I knew there would be no putting this fire out. Not by me anyway.

"The flames seemed to grow larger each second. I stood there mesmerized, staring into the fire. I couldn't seem to move. At one point I heard a voice shouting, 'Lady, get out of there! It's going to explode!' But still I couldn't find my feet. Suddenly, I felt someone grab me by the shoulders, pulling me away from the car to safety. I looked around to see who it was, but no one was there. Then I saw two men running toward the car from different directions, both carrying fire extinguishers. Together, they doused the fire and that was the end of it.

"The car took a month to repair but both Sandy and I were safe. I discovered later that the fuel injection tube had burst, probably the moment I had pushed the pedal to the floor. We thanked God that we escaped the car when we did and that the two men just 'happened' to be in the vicinity, both with fire extinguishers and the nerve to use them. Most of all, I was grateful for invisible hands that had pulled me clear of the fire. When people ask me who it was, I tell them it was my angel. I have little doubt that God had put my guardian angel on special alert that day."

Lord, I thank you for all the times you have protected and watched over me even when I didn't know I needed watching. When I am tempted to be anxious or afraid, help me to remember your faithfulness, realizing that your mercies are new every morning and that your grace is sufficient for each day.

A BETTER GIFT
THAN ANGELS

*"Sir," the invalid replied [to Jesus], "I have no one to help me
into the pool when the water is stirred. While I am trying to
get in, someone else goes down ahead of me." Then Jesus said to
him, "Get up! Pick up your mat and walk." At once the man
was cured; he picked up his mat and walked.*

John 5:7–8

On the east side of Jerusalem were mineral springs that seemed
to possess healing properties. Known as the pool of Bethesda,
the disabled were attracted to it as iron to a magnet. The name,
Bethesda, means "house of mercy" or "house of compassion." The
blind, the lame, and the paralyzed would spend day after day lying
beside the pool, hoping that this would be the day they would be
cured. The Jews believed that an angel of the Lord would come
down from heaven to stir up the waters of the pool. The first person
to enter the water once it moved was invariably healed.

Now Jesus was walking through the area one Sabbath and
noticed a man lying near the pool. This man had been an invalid
for thirty-eight years. When Jesus asked him whether he wanted to
be well, the man assured him that he did, though he had no one to
help him enter the water once it began to stir. Then Jesus simply
told him to stand, pick up his mat, and walk away. And the man
did just that, to everyone's astonishment.

It's interesting to reflect on the man's experience. He must have felt lonely and at a disadvantage. The others had friends and family who could help them get into the pool quickly. But he had no one. His painstaking efforts to drag himself to the pool were always too little, too late. He was never in the right place at the right time to obtain the miracle he desired. Despite these disadvantages, he must still have had hope, for he persisted in coming to the pool. As it turned out, his hope was rewarded, though not in the way he had envisioned.

No one lifted him up, walked over to the pool, and dipped his broken body into the healing waters. Instead, Jesus uttered a simple word of command to put him on his feet again.

Like the invalid at Bethesda, you may be feeling that you are overdue for a miracle. You may have heard stories of people who have traveled across the world to some holy place or who have been prayed with by someone who is said to possess healing powers. You wonder if it's simply a matter of being in the right place at the right time. Like the paralytic, you may feel that you have no one whose prayers will move you closer to a miracle. If so, take heart from this man's story. Despite the long delay, he still hoped that God would have mercy on him. And God did. Rather than sending an angel to heal him, he sent his only Son, a better gift than angels.

Lord, my faith is no faith at all if it depends on whether or not you perform a miracle for me or for someone I love. And yet I believe that miracles do happen. So I ask you to look with compassion on my prayer and to grant the desires of my heart. Whether your answer is yes or no, now or later, I trust that you hear me, that you understand my distress, and that you will act with compassion.

Just a Coincidence?

Are not all angels ministering spirits sent to serve those who will inherit salvation?

Hebrews 1:14

I hate to admit it, but I came of age in the late sixties and early seventies, a peculiar "wrinkle in time" when everything was up for grabs, including the moral values that had shaped my life from day one. Like millions of other college students, I was experimenting with new ideas, new relationships, and a new outlook on life.

In my search for fun and fulfillment, I headed west for a few months to "search for my identity." With three hundred dollars to my name, I embarked on a journey that was to shatter my naiveté and eventually lead me to Christ. But there were many adventures along the way.

One of these took place in San Francisco, where my traveling companion and I landed after several weeks on the road. We were waiting to meet up with another friend who was to arrive a few days later. By then, my three hundred dollars had shrunk to almost nothing. I couldn't even spare enough change for a paperback novel. To save money in that most expensive city, we were staying with friends of friends, who happened to be involved in things that stretched even my worldview.

We spent our first day in a crowded Laundromat, clearing up a backload of dirty wash. It was a dreary job, but somebody had to do it. Suddenly I noticed a small, stoop-shouldered man dragging a cart of books behind him. I spotted the old man through the window as he turned the corner and entered the Laundromat. He advanced steadily until he reached my friend and me. He came to the point right away. Would I like to have a few books, rejects from the Chinatown library? Surprised but pleased, I scooped up an armload, and then he was gone. He had spoken to no one but me and had left as soon as he'd handed me the books. It seemed odd at the time, but I was grateful for something to read at last.

As it turned out, those books were a lifesaver. I was so absorbed in reading them that I had little idea of what was going on in the rest of the apartment. As we pulled out of San Francisco and headed for Los Angeles, my friend described what I had been too absorbed to notice. It seems that a parade of people had been injecting some very big-time drugs in that apartment. Two years later, one of the friends we stayed with died of a drug overdose.

After a short stint in Los Angeles, we arrived in Phoenix, where some friends shared the gospel with me in a powerful new way. It was the beginning of my long road to conversion.

Had an angel walked into the Laundromat that day, with an ingenious method for keeping me out of trouble? Or was my encounter with the little old man simply a coincidence? I don't really know. But I do know that angels are "sent to serve for the sake of those who are to inherit salvation." And though I didn't know it then, I was on my way.

Father, there is no end to your creativity. You invent a million strategies to keep us safe. Thank you for drawing near to me even when I was very far from you. I'm grateful for your angels and for the hidden ways they've watched over me.

An Angel
on an Airplane

Turn to me and be gracious to me,
for I am lonely and afflicted.

Psalm 25:16

Gloria Thompson worked in the sales division of a large firm in the Southwest. A seasoned traveler, she spent many hours in airplanes crisscrossing the country. In the course of her travels, she'd had some interesting encounters with fellow passengers but nothing like the one she was about to experience.

She had just boarded a flight bound for Detroit, when a middle-aged man took his seat beside her. Her gaze rested on him only for an instant, but she had the impression that the man was deeply troubled, despite the smile on his face. She breathed a silent prayer, asking that God would protect him from the temptation to commit suicide. "This is crazy," she thought. "I don't even know the guy. Still, I guess it doesn't hurt to pray."

The plane was about to depart, when he turned and asked whether this was the flight to Duluth. Startled, she replied that it was the flight to Detroit, Michigan, not Duluth, Minnesota. She advised him to check with a flight attendant immediately if he thought he had walked onto the wrong flight. But the man seemed paralyzed by confusion. He explained that he had accepted a job as a regional sales rep for a firm he thought was located in Duluth.

But maybe it was in Detroit. He wasn't sure. He pulled out his ticket, which was written for Detroit. A quick phone call to his new company confirmed that he was on the right flight.

Clearly, the man had problems. He introduced himself as Dick and began to talk freely, perhaps thinking she needed an explanation for his confused behavior. Years earlier, he was diagnosed as being bipolar (at that time it was commonly called manic depression). Now he was at his wit's end. He hadn't eaten in four days and had nowhere to live and no money to live on. His family in Dallas had refused to bail him out one more time, so frustrated were they by his behavior.

Somehow he had landed a job with the firm in Detroit, and they had agreed to fly him in for a few days of orientation. He would have to pay his travel expenses out of his first paycheck. Still, he was uncertain whether to accept the job. Past experience had told him that his depression and anxiety cycled out of control whenever he spent long hours alone on the road, which was exactly what was required in the new job. His therapist had counseled him to remain in Dallas. But he had spurned that advice because living in Dallas would have meant entering a shelter for homeless men. He knew he was running away from his problems, but he felt trapped and desperate. He had never felt as hopeless and afraid as he did that night on the flight to Detroit.

As they talked, he admitted that he had entertained thoughts of suicide. Maybe that would finally put an end to his torment. Gloria spoke with Dick for the duration of the flight and tried to encourage him as best she could. When he asked whether she thought he ought to seek emergency counseling in Detroit, she agreed to help him. He seemed incapable of making a decision on his own. She had planned to spend the weekend with her family, who lived in the area, prior to a week full of meetings in the city.

But she knew she could be flexible about her schedule that Friday night, especially if it meant helping someone in trouble.

It took a few hours to get Dick the kind of help he needed. But she was glad she'd made the effort. On the advice of crisis counselors, he committed himself to a psychiatric hospital in the area, where he received medication to help control his depression and anxiety. In the week that followed, Gloria stayed in touch by phone and visited him in the psychiatric hospital, before returning to her home in Colorado. She was surprised that the hospital staff knew all about her and that the nurses kept telling Dick he had angels watching out for him.

Dick stayed in Detroit for a month. While he was there, two of Gloria's brothers did their best to befriend him. They spent hours talking with him, encouraging him to face his problems. Reluctantly, Dick returned to Dallas to face the music. When he did, one of his brothers met him at the bus station. With the help of his brother and a friend who lent him some money to help him get back on his feet, Dick was able to find a place to live, which was decidedly better than being out on the street.

Since then, Dick and Gloria have spoken on the phone several times. Not surprisingly, Dick has had his ups and downs. Gloria knows he isn't out of the woods by any stretch of the imagination. Though she doesn't know whether Dick will be able to turn his life around, she hopes he has at least turned an important corner. Of one thing she is certain, though: God has turned a needy stranger into a friend for whom she will continue to pray.

When Gloria returned home from her trip to Detroit, she thought about what had happened on the plane that day. She had prayed for a stranger, not knowing that God would invite her and her two brothers to become part of the answer to that prayer. Later, when she visited Dick in the psychiatric ward before returning home, she noticed that he wore a small angel pin on the collar of his shirt. When Dick explained that a passenger on the previous flight had given it to him, she couldn't help but smile. Wasn't it just like God to send a token of his love! No matter what Dick would face in the days and months ahead, she knew that heavenly protectors wouldn't be far away.

Father, I'm amazed that you weave us into the fabric of your miracles. So often, you funnel your help through us, rather than pushing us aside to accomplish your purposes. As we intercede, may we be willing to become part of the answer to our prayer for others, no matter how hopeless the situation. Ultimately, Lord, the outcome is in your hands.

9

WHEN NO DELIVERING ANGEL COMES

No wound? No scar?
Yet, as the Master shall the servant be,
And pierced are the feet that follow Me;
But thine are whole; can he have followed far
Who has no wound or scar?

Amy Carmichael

R are is the person who has not suffered some tragedy in life. We all know women who have been raped, men who have died of horrible diseases, children who have been abused, soldiers who have been mutilated in war. Why don't the angels come to straighten things out? Surely they have the power. Where are they when we really need them?

Anyone who believes that angels exist will certainly pose this question. Of course it is really just another form of the age-old question about good and evil. How could a good God allow evil to exist?

The answer is not simple. Part of it lies in the nature of love itself. We learn from Scripture that God is love. When he created us, he took all the risks that love demands. By this I mean that he fashioned us as beings who would be capable of either embracing or rejecting his love. Robots cannot love, but men and women can. By the same token, they can also hate. This was the tremendous risk God took in creating us as beings capable of either embracing or rejecting his love.

Evil is merely the refusal to love God. Each person makes that choice here on earth. Whenever and wherever God is spurned, evil fills our cities, our streets, and our homes. Even so, God can turn such evil on its head, compelling it to serve his purposes.

Ultimately, that is what we see in the life, death, and resurrection of Jesus of Nazareth. We see the deeper love of God triumphing despite the evil intentions of fallen angels and human beings. As we confront evil in our own lives and in the lives of those we love, we must remember that God is for us and that he will never abandon or forsake us. Ultimately, his love is a power that conquers every evil and vanquishes every foe.

HOW TO FIGHT
THE DARK ANGELS

*Then Jesus was led by the Spirit into the desert to be tempted
by the devil. After fasting forty days and forty nights, he was
hungry. The tempter came to him.... Then the devil left him,
and angels came and attended him.*

Matthew 4:1–3, 11

After Jesus' baptism in the Jordan River, the Spirit led him into
the wilderness to be tempted by the devil. Jesus fasted for forty
days and nights in the barren wilderness, and then the devil arrived
to tempt him three times.

Isn't it interesting that Jesus deliberately weakened himself
before engaging in combat with his archenemy, Satan? He fasted
forty days and nights, and he was starving. In a sense, you could say
that he made his body weak to make his spirit strong. So often the
methods of heaven contradict our most basic instincts.

Notice too that the Spirit actually led Jesus into the wilderness. Jesus didn't decide on his own that it was time to take on
the devil, but he allowed the Holy Spirit to initiate a season in his
life in which he would endure testing and temptation. Moreover,
the angels didn't appear on the scene until Jesus had successfully
resisted every trick Satan threw at him. Only then did the heavenly
host come and wait on him, much like a prize-fighter's attendants
after a fight.

At times, the Spirit will also lead us into the wilderness to endure a time of trial. It may be a wilderness of loneliness, illness, misunderstanding, poverty, failure, or doubt. Whatever the case, we can take courage from this crucial episode in Jesus' life. For Jesus' wilderness experience actually prepared him for his public ministry. The miracles, the preaching, the healings would all characterize the most tremendous ministry the world had ever seen. But not before Jesus engaged in a fierce and terrible spiritual combat.

If you find yourself in the wilderness, perhaps you should be encouraged. God may be preparing you for a time of greater fruitfulness and joy. Such times often do not emerge without a struggle. That struggle may involve facing your own sinfulness and lack of faith. Your enemy wants to convince you that God has abandoned you and that you are good for nothing. You may long for angels to whisper "courage" in your ears, but none comes. In this kind of desert, remember to cling to God. Just as Jesus prayed and fasted, keeping in vital communion with his Father, make sure that you are holding fast to God in the midst of your wilderness experience. You can't possibly face evil on your own and win. But with patience and faith you can emerge stronger and more hopeful than before.

At times you will be tempted to escape the wilderness. If you're lonely, you might find yourself rationalizing an unhealthy relationship. If you're anxious about the future, you might become obsessed with finding ways to protect yourself and your family from financial hardship. If you haven't been able to bear children, you might be tempted to try medical treatments you believe to be unethical in order to conceive. Whatever your temptations, resist the enemy and ask God for the strength to go on.

There will be an end to your wilderness, a time when the angels will come and wait on you as they did on Jesus. That will be a time of rejoicing, a time of moving once again in power and confidence, a time of blessing as God continues to fulfill his purpose for your life.

> *Help me, God. I am so tired of this wilderness. Sometimes I think it will never end. I feel so needy that I don't like what I see in the mirror. Are you really testing me? If so, what am I supposed to be learning? Help me to cling to you, Lord, and strengthen me against the temptations of self-pity and fear. Lead me to a place of safety.*

A Dream or
a Nightmare?

Joseph had a dream, and when he told it to his brothers, they
hated him all the more. He said to them, "Listen to this dream
I had: We were binding sheaves of grain out in the field when
suddenly my sheaf rose and stood upright, while your sheaves
gathered around mine and bowed down to it."

Genesis 37:5–7

At seventeen, Joseph was the favorite son of the patriarch Jacob
and the least favorite brother of his ten half-brothers. Perhaps
it was youthful naiveté that led him to share a dream that would
only pour fuel on the fire of their hatred.

Before long, his glorious dream had given birth to a living nightmare. Still chafing from the insult, the brothers spotted him one
day in the field and said to each other, "Here comes that dreamer.
Let's get rid of him once and for all. Then we'll see what comes of
his dreams." Instead of murdering him, they decided to sell him for
eight ounces of silver to some Midianite traders en route to Egypt.
The once-favored son had become a slave in a foreign country. His
dream, it seemed, was nothing more than a childish fantasy.

But in fact, the dream was unfolding even in the midst of
Joseph's enslavement and imprisonment. Circumstances eventually brought him to the attention of Pharaoh himself, who gave
him great powers over his kingdom. Before long, Joseph's brothers

came begging for bread in the midst of a severe famine. When they did, Scripture says, "They bowed down to him with their faces to the ground" (Genesis 42:6). After years of trial and hardship, the dream was finally fulfilled and Joseph was able to provide refuge for his father and his brothers in a season of famine.

The seventeen-year-old Joseph couldn't have known that his dream was only part of the picture—the happy ending to a story that would have more than its share of tragic twists and turns. Though Joseph lived thousands of years ago, his experience is still fresh for those who understand it.

Like Joseph, we have been given grace to know the conclusion of the story—the happy ending that awaits those who love God. Still, God doesn't reveal everything that will happen to us along the way. We are yet living between the dream and its fulfillment. We know that Christ has conquered all our enemies, even death, and yet we experience many small deaths each day. We still sin, we still hurt one another, we still suffer from unfulfilled longings. When we are tempted to think that faith is nothing but a childish fantasy, let us remember Joseph's story and take heart. He didn't abandon the dream and neither can we.

Father, you work in mysterious ways, often in ways that confound human wisdom. The more I know of you, the more I realize there is to know. Help me to remember that you give us dreams at night, in the midst of darkness. Let those dreams strengthen me, especially when I am living through a particularly dark time in my life. Let me hold on to the dream and live it out in the power of your Spirit.

AN ANGEL OF COURAGE

Jesus went out as usual to the Mount of Olives, and his disciples followed him. On reaching the place, he said to them, "Pray that you will not fall into temptation." He withdrew about a stone's throw beyond them, knelt down and prayed, "Father, if you are willing, take this cup from me; yet not my will, but yours be done." An angel from heaven appeared to him and strengthened him.

Luke 22:39–43

Sometimes we make the mistake of thinking it was easy for Jesus to die for us. After all, he was God, wasn't he? He could do anything he wanted. Yet the Gospels tell us that Jesus was filled with agony and fear on the evening before his death, so much so that he asked his Father to change his mind about the crucifixion — to save him from the "cup of suffering" he was destined to drink.

It grieves me to imagine what Jesus must have endured for my sake. Yet it also comforts me. He felt the same fear that prowls inside my soul whenever awful possibilities lurk. Like Jesus, I can honestly cry out to God and ask him to rescue me. And like Jesus, I can tell the Father that whatever happens, I want his will to be done.

The Father answered his Son, not with the response Jesus hoped for but with the answer he was willing to receive. Instead of a delivering angel, God sent an angel to impart greater courage for the terrible ordeal ahead.

For his part, Jesus urged the disciples to pray they would not fall into temptation. Despite his urging, they couldn't stay awake long enough to pray with him in that dark hour. They had just eaten the heavy Passover meal and drunk the Passover wine. How could Jesus expect them to stay awake and pray? What kind of temptation was Jesus talking about anyway?

Jesus knew that fear would rule his disciples for a time. After his arrest, Satan would appear to be ascendant. Peter, James, John, and the rest of the lot would lose faith, betray him, and run and hide. None of them would stand when the soldiers came to seize him.

We wonder how the disciples could have been such cowards. Yet we succumb to the same temptations they did. Like Peter, we tell Jesus that we love him and that we are willing to follow him anywhere. Yet we are unwilling to follow him into the darkness of fear and confusion and suffering, unwilling to believe that God will send his angels to give us courage to face the most terrible circumstances. Our faith trembles when disaster looms. We want to withdraw, to run and hide, to find a place of ultimate safety.

At such times, we need to echo Jesus' prayer. "I'm afraid, Lord. Please take this suffering from me. Even so, Father, don't answer my prayer if it contradicts your will." As we pray, God will answer us. Whether or not he spares us from the suffering we most fear, he will give us courage to face whatever comes.

Lord, you test me and often find me wanting. Sometimes I am shocked by the cowardice you uncover in me. But just as the angel strengthened you on the Mount of Olives, give me the strength to stand firm no matter what the Father asks.

CALLING ALL ANGELS

Do you think I cannot call on my Father, and he will at once put at my disposal more than twelve legions of angels? But how then would the Scriptures be fulfilled that say it must happen in this way?

Matthew 26:53–54

Picture the scene. It is the eve of the crucifixion. Jesus has just been seized in the garden of Gethsemane by the soldiers of the chief priests and elders. Peter, always the leader among the disciples and a man of action, strikes the slave of the high priest, cutting off his ear. He is willing to defend Jesus to the death if need be. And then Jesus rebukes him.

A deeper logic is at work, a divine plan that throws Peter and the disciples into confusion. A battle to the death they can understand, but surrender in the face of such manifest evil? Never! And so they flee.

Reading about Peter always comforts me. He meant well, but he often made a mess of things, sometimes embarrassingly so. Yet Jesus loved him and confided in him. If it had been up to me in that dark confrontation in Gethsemane, I would have screamed loud and clear for as many legions of angels as the Father could spare. My top priority would have been to get everyone out of there alive, especially Jesus and me. I would have been like Peter, taking things into my own hands in order to avert disaster and ensure that the Messiah would eventually be crowned the king of Israel.

Yet Jesus, who never acts predictably, rebukes Peter. He knows that fear, rather than the fury of the high priests and their soldiers, is his real enemy. Jesus could have summoned an angel cavalry to the rescue, but that would have meant undermining his Father's plan. True, there would have been no agonizing crucifixion, but neither would there have been a glorious resurrection. You and I would still be alienated from God and enslaved by our enemy. Jesus refrains from calling on the power of the angels so that a deeper power could be at work, a power of obedience, of love, and of lamb-like acceptance of the plan and purpose of God.

Father, as the heavens are higher than the earth, so are your ways higher than my ways and your thoughts higher than mine. I confess that I am so often puzzled by the way you do things, the prayers you agree with and the ones you don't. But you are the Lord. Don't let me cling to my ways over yours. Help me to let go and trust you.

FEELING
ABANDONED BY GOD

~~~

My God, my God, why have you forsaken me?

Matthew 27:46

The anguished cry of Jesus from the cross resounds across the centuries to fill our own hearts with almost unbearable grief. How is it that the Son of God, the one who breathed life into creation, was apparently conquered by death and abandoned by his Father?

Is this love, we ask? Jesus himself assured us that no earthly father would give a stone to a son who asked for bread. Yet wasn't his heavenly Father giving Jesus precisely that—a silence so stony hard as to seem like complete abandonment? Couldn't God have broken the terrifying silence with a word of encouragement as he did when Jesus was baptized in the Jordan: "This is my Son, whom I love; with him I am well pleased" (Matthew 3:17)? But the Father said nothing as Jesus hung naked on a Roman cross.

Sometimes we too feel this seemingly heartless absence of God in our lives. Where is he when a child dies, when we lose a job, suffer the pain of divorce, or feel betrayed by a fellow believer? On a larger scale, where was God when the Jews were gassed at Auschwitz?

If God isn't willing to take away suffering, couldn't he at least reassure us in the midst of it? We desperately want to know that somehow all will be well. Of course, God often does speak to us in such circumstances, but what about the times he doesn't?

Clearly, the cost of our redemption involved tremendous inner agony as well as excruciating physical pain. And yet Jesus, uttering this heart cry, was actually repeating the first verse of Psalm 22: "My God, my God, why have you forsaken me?" By doing so, he was calling forth the words of the entire psalm. If we stop with the first verse, we fail to plumb the depths of Christ's faith in his Father, even in the midst of his suffering.

Psalm 22 continues later, saying, "You who fear the LORD, praise him! All you offspring of Jacob glorify him; stand in awe of him all you offspring of Israel! For he did not despise or abhor the affliction of the afflicted; he did not hide his face from me, but heard when I cried to him" (vv. 23–24 NRSV).

Nailed to a cross, suffering a horrible death, Jesus did not deny his feeling of abandonment. His cry was an honest one. Even so, he affirmed with utter certainty his faith in the Father's goodness and in the purpose of his plan. God's ways are often so utterly foreign to us that we sometimes feel repulsed by them. Why did a good man die so that I could go free? Part of the answer to the age-old question regarding evil in the world has to do with the evil in you and me. The remedy for our sin is so radical that it startles and sometimes shames us. Through obedience, Jesus liberated us from our sin and guilt.

In the most desperate hour of his life, no angel came to deliver him or even to offer words of comfort. Yet we know that the resurrection of Jesus displayed the deeper love and faithfulness of God.

Perhaps you are facing some kind of death in your life. It may be the death of a dream or the death of a relationship or the very real death of someone you love. Remember to pray all of Psalm 22, not just the first line, for "God hears you when you cry to him."

Father, why have you abandoned me? I cry out to you but hear nothing in response. Why do you stay so far away from me? Yet you are the One who has kept me safe from the moment of my birth. Somehow, I know that you do not despise my afflictions, but you hear me when I call to you. Because of you, I will live to tell others of your faithfulness.

10

ANGELS AT THE MOMENT OF OUR DEATH

✍

Do not rejoice over a ship that is setting out to sea,
for you cannot know what storms it may encounter....
But rejoice rather over a ship that has reached port
and brings home all its passengers in peace.

Adapted from the Talmud

For each of us, death is a destination we cannot avoid. It represents the ultimate challenge to our faith, the end of the world as we know it. Despite all the talk of "death with dignity," there is usually little dignity in our experience of dying. It is a time of letting go, of weakness, of humbling—a time when we can no longer ignore the limits of our humanity.

Jesus himself wept at the death of his best friend Lazarus, this despite the fact that he would soon raise him from the dead. No matter what anybody tells you, death is no friend of ours. To make matters worse, death involves a journey we make without any other human companion. We go it alone, except, that is, for the Lord and his angels.

The Bible indicates that angels are present, conveying the souls of men and women from this world into the next. By way of example, remember that angels carried the soul of the poor man Lazarus to heaven and were also present at the tomb of Jesus. Billy Graham assures us about the role of angels when he says, "Hundreds of accounts record the heavenly escort of angels at death. When my maternal grandmother died, for instance, the room seemed to fill up with a heavenly light. She sat up in bed and almost laughingly said, 'I see Jesus. He has his arms outstretched toward me. I see Ben [her husband] and I see the angels.'"

A friend of mine told me about her mother's death from cancer. "My mother died two years ago. She actually came to the Lord during the time of her illness. The night she died, my sister was near her bed. She was astonished to see my mother surrounded by a brilliant light. She said it looked like the aurora borealis. She was sure it was the angels."

If you fear death, you can take tremendous comfort that you and those you love will not have to make the journey alone. God in his tender love will never abandon those who belong to him. He will surround you with his angels to keep you from harm and lead you safely home.

THE ANGEL IN THE TOMB

So Joseph bought some linen cloth, took down the body, wrapped it in the linen, and placed it in a tomb cut out of rock. Then he rolled a stone against the entrance of the tomb.... As [Mary Magdalene and Mary the mother of James, and Salome] entered the tomb, they saw a young man dressed in a white robe sitting on the right side.

Mark 15:46; 16:5

Joseph was a rich man from Arimathea and a somewhat secret follower of Jesus. While Jesus' body dangled lifelessly on the cross, Joseph went to Pilate to request that he be allowed to bury him. So he wrapped the body in a linen cloth and laid it tenderly in his own tomb, which had recently been hewn from the rock.

He had heard Jesus' last words: "It is finished" (John 19:30). Joseph supposed that it was indeed finished as he rolled a large stone across the entrance of the tomb and returned home to grieve for his dead friend. The best hope of Israel had been laid to rest on a cold slab of stone.

How could Joseph have known that his own tomb would soon be utterly transformed by the power of God? When he heard the rumor of the angel at the tomb, he must have rushed to see for himself. Did he crush the linen cloth between his fingers, the death wrap that he had himself wound around the body of Jesus? Did he question Mary Magdalene about the angel's exact words: "Do not be alarmed.... You are looking for Jesus the Nazarene, who was crucified. He has risen! He is not here" (Mark 16:6).

Every one of us can take comfort from the fact that Jesus was raised from the dead in the tomb of another man. It is as though the dead Jesus was laid to rest in our own graves. Because he trusted in the Father, he submitted to the terrible power of death. And God, through a greater power, raised him to life as the firstborn of the new creation.

One day we too will know the chill of death. The thought of it frightens us. But we can take courage, as Joseph must have, from knowing that Jesus was laid to rest in our graves first. Just as death could not hold him in its grip, it will not be able to hold us. Like Jesus, we will be raised to a new life. And the angel will say to those at the grave, "Why do you seek the living among the dead?"

Father, I ask that at the hour of my death, you will comfort me with the knowledge that Jesus was laid to rest in my grave first. Just as death had no power to hold him, so it will have no power to hold me. In that moment, may I proclaim with Paul, "Where, O death, is your victory? Where, O death, is your sting?" (1 Corinthians 15:55).

AUNT KATE
AND THE ANGELS

*Even though I walk
    through the valley of the shadow of death,
I will fear no evil,
    for you are with me;
your rod and your staff,
    they comfort me.*

Psalm 23:4

Wayne Herring is a Presbyterian pastor in Memphis, Tennessee; he knows that angels sometimes show up just when we need them most.

"My aunt, Kate Lewis, loved Christ all her life. She and my uncle had no children of their own, and my aunt treated me like her own son. On the day I announced my intention to enter the ministry, no one in my family rejoiced at the prospect — except my Aunt Kate, that is. She was thrilled and promised to pray faithfully for me. Her faith and love made such an impression that I eventually named one of my daughters after her.

"Five years ago my aunt lay dying of congestive heart failure. In her late eighties, her frail body was no match for the disease. Her struggle with death was prolonged and agonizing. She was gasping for breath and had been semi-comatose for many days. At one point the nurses actually tried to revive her by initiating some heroic measures to prolong her life. My father was at my aunt's bedside when it happened. Suddenly Aunt Kate sat straight up and looked around at everyone in the room. Her eyes were sharp and her speech clear, but she wasn't happy. 'Why on earth did you bring me back?' she scolded. 'It's been wonderful. I've been with the angels and I didn't want to leave!' These were her last words. She sank back down on her pillow, and a few days later she was gone."

Like Kate Lewis, all of us will one day make the journey from this life to the next. Most of us are apprehensive about our deaths. What will it be like to stand on the edge of what has been called the ultimate frontier? How will we endure the emotional and physical suffering that death often entails? We wonder, after all, whether there really is anything on the other side. Will we close our eyes never to open them again? Is death a massive black hole from which we will never emerge?

Aunt Kate hadn't wanted to come back even for a few moments, let alone a few days. But maybe God allowed her to return for our sakes. We need reassurance about the difficult transition from this life to the next. Most of us prefer the hard dirt of earth to the white clouds of heaven. This world may be far from perfect, but at least it's a world we know. When the time comes for our journey toward eternity, we need reassurance that we and those we love will not be left to make the trip alone. At the moment we die, God will send an escort of angels to convey our souls safely into paradise. Anyone who loves God and belongs to his Son will one day stand in his presence, enjoying his company forever. Who knows? Kate Lewis may even be standing by the gate, ready to greet us when we get there.

Lord, I admit that I am afraid to die. I've seen the face of death in hospitals and funeral homes, and it's not pretty.

Because your Spirit lives in me, I know that you will give me an eternity of days to spend with you. Give me courage to make the journey when the time comes. Then send your angels to carry me swiftly to your loving arms.

CAN'T YOU SEE THE ANGELS?

⥈

The time came when the beggar died and the angels carried him to Abraham's side.

Luke 16:22

Joann Kruse's cousin suffered from leukemia as a young child. "I can't remember a time when Catherine wasn't sick. I always felt so sorry for her. She could never do all the fun things other kids could.

"My Uncle Ray and Aunt Delores had both been raised in Christian homes, but they had left their faith behind many years earlier. They seemed bitter and didn't want to have anything to do with the church. They even seemed estranged from the rest of the family. When Catherine became ill, they had such a hard time coping.

"Poor Catherine was frightened of dying and my aunt and uncle didn't know what to say to comfort her. Finally, a family friend began to talk to her about God and his angels. He told Catherine that God loved her very much, so much so that he had provided angels to watch over her. When the time came for her to make the journey to heaven, the angels would be there to keep her safe, he told her.

"I remember the year Catherine turned ten. It was the beginning of the end. She became so weak that she couldn't even sit up in bed anymore. While my aunt and uncle were keeping vigil one afternoon at her bedside, she shocked them by suddenly sitting straight up and pointing. 'Can't you see the angels? They're all around us!' she said excitedly.

"Uncle Ray asked her what the angels were doing. 'They're laughing and one of them is stretching out his arms and asking me if I would like to go with them,' the little girl replied.

" 'Would you like to go?' my uncle asked.

" 'If it's all right with you and Mom,' she replied. It must have broken their hearts, but both parents nodded their assent, and Catherine stretched out her small arms, reaching toward invisible hands. The very next instant, she was gone.

"Uncle Ray and Aunt Delores were never the same after that. Catherine's vision and the peace and joy that accompanied her death marked the beginning of their return to faith and their reconciliation with the rest of our family. In fact, Uncle Ray is the one who told me the story of Catherine's death. Both of them are gone now. I can't help but think how glad they must be to be back in each other's arms, surrounded by the angels who took such good care of them here on earth."

Father, you are the Author of life. You give life and you take it away. Thank you for creating each of us, for knitting us together in our mothers' wombs. Indeed, we are fearfully and wonderfully made. Before we are born, you know the story of our lives. You have numbered every one of our days before even one of them exists. Watch over us, Lord, and watch over our children. When the time comes, carry us home safely, borne on the wings of angels.

ON THE SIDE
OF THE ANGELS?

*They shouted, "This is the voice of a god, not of a man."
Immediately, because Herod did not give praise to God, an
angel of the Lord struck him down, and he was eaten by
worms and died.*

Acts 12:22–23

So far, we've been telling consoling stories about angels and how
they help us at the moment of death. It's important to realize,
however, that the good angels aren't always sweetness and light to
everyone they meet.

In this case from the Bible, an angel actually caused the death of
a man who had for years been opposing God. King Herod Agrippa
had killed James, the brother of John. He had also taken Peter pris-
oner, but, as we know, an angel came and freed him before Herod
could do him the intended harm.

Like Herod the Great and Herod Antipas before him, Herod
Agrippa did his best to oppose the spread of the gospel so that he
could consolidate his own power. What Herod failed to realize
was that he was opposing more than mere flesh and blood. He had
taken his stand on the wrong side of the angels—an extremely
dangerous place to be. The end for this wretched man came when
he allowed people to worship him as God. Imagine his terror when
his body was devoured by a repulsive and horrible disease.

Scripture shows the angels ministering God's judgment nearly as frequently as they carry his messages. Much as we would like to, we simply cannot tame the angels, just as we cannot tame God. They are loving to those who love God and terrible to those who oppose him.

As God's people, we can rejoice in all the works that the angels perform. What kind of God would let evil go unopposed forever? The believers in Jerusalem must have been glad that their enemy could no longer do them harm. Evil men and women who refuse to repent need to face the consequences of their deeds.

But we also must realize that God is the only one who can pronounce judgment. Until he does, our task is to continue to pray for our enemies. If we do, we will be certain to stand on the side of the angels.

Father, you remind us that vengeance belongs to you alone. I thank you that you are just and that you do not allow evil to go unpunished. Lord, I pray for those who seem captivated by evil, those who kill and brutalize and live only for themselves. Help them to repent so that they will know your mercy rather than your wrath.

ARE YOU READY TO SEE AN ANGEL?

... so that through death he [Jesus] might destroy the one who has the power of death, that is, the devil, and free those who all their lives were held in slavery by the fear of death. For it is clear that he did not come to help angels, but the descendants of Abraham.

Hebrews 2:14 – 16 NRSV

We hear a lot these days about near-death experiences. Some people believe they are caused by chemical reactions in the brain. Others believe they are authentic spiritual experiences. Still others suspect they are satanic deceptions foisted on the gullible. Such things are often difficult to discern, but my theory is that some of the visions are authentic while others are deceptive, and only wisdom can tell the difference.

I have another pet theory and that is that everybody should be blessed with at least one Aunt Betty in their lives. I live near a small town that even has an Aunt Betty's Restaurant. Most of my friends have an Aunt Betty tucked away somewhere in their family. My own Aunt Betty was my mother's only sister. If you don't have an Aunt Betty, I'm sorry for you.

Anyway, my Aunt Betty was the kind of aunt who always showed up with huge cookies, fresh from the bakery. She was my mother's best friend and my favorite aunt. So it was heartbreaking to hear the news that cancer had spread throughout her body and that she had only a few months to live.

My aunt wasn't a particularly religious woman. She lived her life as many people do, focused on family and friends, but not especially aware of the spiritual dimension of life—or so it seemed to me. As time went on, the disease got the upper hand and my aunt had to be hospitalized. At one point, she had a vision that she later confided to her physician and to my mother. It seems she was walking in the direction of a being who was radiating light, but she was terrified to draw any closer to this being.

When her doctor heard the story, he told her that there was nothing to fear. If it happened again, she should keep walking toward the light. But I wasn't so sure. Many people who claim to have had a near-death experience describe feelings of peace and joy in the presence of this "being of light." Why was my aunt so afraid? I wondered if her fear came from the fact that she wasn't yet ready to die.

As it happened, she hung on for a couple of months, and my mother and I were able to share our faith with her. My aunt prayed a prayer committing her life to the Lord shortly before she died.

My aunt's passing was anything but easy, but I pray that when she left, she was ready to see the angel of the Lord. I believe that God had mercy on her and gave her the chance to surrender her life to him before it was too late. Though she suffered greatly, her disease allowed her time to make her peace with God. When the angel of death came for the final time, I hope she met him unafraid.

Jesus, you didn't die for the angels but for us. I ask that you will pour out your grace unstintingly to those in my family who have not yet surrendered their lives to you. Spare them no suffering that will be necessary for them to come to a saving knowledge of you. Reveal yourself to them while there is yet time. Stretch out the long arms of your mercy and bring them into your kingdom.

11

WITH THE ANGELS ON OUR SIDE

❦

I said to the man who stood at the gate of the year,
"Give me a light that I may tread safely into the unknown."
And he replied, "Go out into the darkness and put your hand
into the hand of God. That shall be to you better than light
and safer than a known way."

Minnie Louise Haskins

The angels have played a part in our past and in our present, and they will certainly play an important role in our future. We don't know the challenges we will face tomorrow morning let alone next year or the year after. But God does, and he can set his angels in motion on our behalf.

Perhaps they will come with a word of encouragement, or with an exhortation to repentance, or with a call that only we can fulfill. They may carry answers to our prayers from the very throne of God. They may show themselves to us in dreams. Whatever happens, we know that if we love Christ, we will have the angels on our side.

How can we go wrong when the angels are rooting for us? Try to remember this the next time you face some kind of unfolding disaster, the next time you make a major decision, the next time you pray for God's intervention. We may yet suffer many indignities in this life, but the truth is we are destined for a life of eternal bliss.

Meanwhile, the angels are part of God's provision to help us through the snares of this world. In the service of Christ, they can keep our souls intact and our future secure. Right now they have their work cut out for them, but one day, when we are at last home safe, the angels will breathe a sigh of relief, put their feet up, and take a well-deserved vacation, knowing that they can spend the rest of eternity savoring the memory of a job well done.

Eavesdropping on Angels

⟡

Then I looked and heard the voice of many angels.

Revelation 5:11

K athy Deering has never seen an angel, but she's pretty sure she overheard two angels conversing in the middle of the night. "I felt I should talk to a friend about a concern I had regarding her life but was afraid of broaching the subject. Should I say something? Should I just keep quiet? Maybe I was being a busybody, but if I didn't talk to her, who would? I kept going back and forth in my mind. The more I prayed, the stronger my conviction that I should get up the nerve to tell my friend what was worrying me, so I set up a time to meet with her.

"That night a small noise woke me. I listened with my eyes closed. (I didn't bother opening them because I can't see a thing without my glasses anyway.) From the corner of my bedroom, I heard two soft voices. One said, 'Is she really going to do it?'

"'Yes!' replied the other.

"Somehow, I knew that the conversation I was overhearing concerned my decision to speak with my friend. I fell asleep again and awoke with the conviction and courage I needed to be honest with her. As it turned out, she really appreciated my frankness and everything worked out really well. Later she told me that her life was changed as a result of our conversation.

"I'm convinced that the voices I heard belonged to angels. Maybe my guardian angel was actually conversing with hers. I don't really know. All I know is that their words gave me the courage I needed, the last shove over the edge, so that I was able to do what God wanted."

Kathy's story assures us that the angels are involved in our lives. They care about the decisions we make and stand by to help us. We may be uncertain about a direction we should take, a decision we should make, a difficult conversation we should initiate. If we surrender these things in prayer, we can be confident that God will help us discern the right course of action. He may give us a growing sense that one choice is better than another. He may increase our courage to take risks. He may present us with several good possibilities from which we are free to choose. Along the way, we may stumble a bit, but with the angels on our side, we needn't worry about making any fatal mistakes.

Father, sometimes I wish I could hear you more clearly. I'm not always sure what to do. Even so, you know that I want to live my life in a way that pleases and delights you. Sharpen my hearing, Lord, so that you won't have to shout to get my attention. Let me listen to the still, small voice that speaks to me of your love and of your will.

PUT A SMILE
ON YOUR ANGEL'S FACE

I tell you, there is rejoicing in the presence of the angels of God over one sinner who repents.

Luke 15:10

The angels get excited whenever men and women begin to face the truth about themselves. They know that ever since Adam and Eve, we have been playing hide-and-seek with God and with each other, afraid to face the darkness in our own hearts and unwilling to admit our desperate need for God's forgiveness. Because the angels love us, they want to see us reconciled to the source of all joy, to God himself. But they know this is impossible until we are honest about our true condition.

This honesty is rare and painful, little evidenced in our world. The nightly news regales us with a parade of victims and victimizers: one political party points the finger at another; hideous crimes are rationalized because the perpetrators were once victims; rivalries between public figures are celebrated in television miniseries. Surrounded by a culture in which "nobody is to blame," we find it hard to face up to the wrongs we inflict on others. Secretly, we may despise ourselves for our faults and failings, but we display a defiant face to the world.

Fortunately, God never falls for our ruses. Instead, he presses in on us, hoping that we will turn to him and tell him we're tired of pretense, that we've had enough, that we can't seem to become the kind of people we want to be. That is what repentance is all about: turning toward God and away from sin. As we turn to God, we will find him utterly more attractive than the evil magnetism of sin. As we humble ourselves, he will draw near.

It is true that we are both sinners and sinned against. As such, we are victims of other people's wrongdoing. Even so, we are responsible for our own sinful reactions to those who inflict harm on us. We can either choose to perpetuate the deforming power of sin by responding in kind or we can snap the cycle through forgiveness. Our future happiness depends on the choice we make.

God treats us, after all, with tremendous dignity. He will not demean us by assenting to the lie that we are incapable of changing. He will not degrade us by stripping us of personal responsibility. True, if we insist, he will allow us to carry on the pretense that we aren't really that bad and that we can handle our lives well enough on our own.

But if we want to put a smile on an angel's face, we must stop hiding the truth about ourselves from ourselves. We must begin to realize that God already knows the worst about us and loves us anyway. We can then realize that the angels themselves are rejoicing over us, the one sinner who repents.

Father, even remorse is your gift. Help me to admit the spiritual sickness that I struggle with, and then give me a soul-deep sorrow for my sin. May it be the kind of sorrow that causes me to run to you for healing, rather than the kind that makes me flee from you in fear. May my repentance be a catalyst for healing—a promise of a future filled with your mercy and loving-kindness.

A WING AND A PRAYER

❧

[Gabriel] came and said to me, "Daniel, I have now come
out to give you wisdom and understanding. At the beginning
of your supplications a word went out, and I have come to
declare it, for you are greatly beloved. So consider the word
and understand the vision."

Daniel 9:22–23 NRSV

The Jewish people had ignored repeated warnings to turn away
from their sin or face the consequences. Obstinate in their
disregard for God, these stiff-necked people were finally conquered
by one of the ancient world's most powerful nations: Babylon. As a
result, Daniel and many others like him were forced into captivity,
exiled from their beloved Jerusalem.

But Daniel never sulked or complained about his predica-
ment, insisting that he was being punished unfairly. Instead, he
knelt before God and beseeched him to have mercy on his people.
Though Daniel had not himself participated in the sin of God's
people, he stood with those who had, humbling himself and repent-
ing of their sin. Evidently, God could not resist the prayers of such a
man. The angel Gabriel actually told Daniel that a word went out
from heaven because of his prayer. And when God speaks a word,
things begin to happen. Incredible as it seems, we learn from this
story that our prayers can actually set heaven in motion. Some-

times they even have the power to dispatch angels with a message of wisdom.

Much of the world today is engulfed in spiritual blindness, obstinate in its disregard for God. All of us, believers and unbelievers, are suffering the consequences of this failure to live in obedience. The local news disgorges stories that horrify and depress us. Murder, child abuse, gang violence, rape—this is the standard fare many of us wake up to each morning. Our families are ripped apart by bitter divorces. Our children can't seem to find their way. We feel a gnawing sense of tension and anxiety as we attempt to cope with life on these terms. The truth is that our culture is dying of its sins, of its arrogance, of its failure to admit the need for God's mercy.

As Christians, we may feel it's unfair that we are consigned to such a world. After all, we may not be perfect people but at least we are trying to live in a way that honors God. But complaining merely wastes God's time and ours. We are in the midst of this mess for a reason: to share the light that lives in us, a light that is far stronger than the darkness that threatens. Like Daniel, let us fall to our knees, acknowledging our sins, begging God's mercy, and identifying with the stiff-necked people around us. As we do, we might even find we have a few kinks of our own to work out.

God can't possibly resist the prayers of the humble. If we turn to him and beg for his mercy, he may send out a powerful word that will set us on a new course and stop the cultural slide we have been experiencing for so many years. Daniel's prayers got Gabriel moving. Maybe the angels are standing by, ready to bring us a word in response to our prayers, a word that will impart a deeper vision and fill us with a more vivid and unshakable hope for the future.

O God, you have been patient with us though we have turned from your light and descended into darkness. I am not foolish enough to come before you on account of my own integrity. Instead, I come before you because of your great mercy. O Lord, hear; O Lord, forgive; O Lord, listen and act and have mercy on us!

WHEN AN ANGEL
CALLS YOUR NAME

*When the angel of the LORD appeared to Gideon, he said,
"The LORD is with you, mighty warrior." ... "But Lord,"
Gideon asked, "how can I save Israel? My clan is the weakest
in Manasseh, and I am the least in my family."*

Judges 6:12, 15

Gideon was a farmer—and not a successful one at that. Every time he or any other Israelite would plant a crop, their enemies, the Midianites, would swoop down on them and destroy it. He was hardly a tough guy, and yet the angel called him a mighty warrior. Gideon responded as you or I might have: "Who, me? You must be kidding!"

But the angel commissioned Gideon to save Israel from their enemies. Gideon still doubted, so he asked God to give him a sign to confirm his word, and God did. Despite all odds, he fulfilled the call God had placed on his life. At one point, he led a mere three hundred men against a horde of enemies and defeated them. The angel knew what he was talking about when he called Gideon a mighty warrior.

God has created each of us for a purpose. Our primary purpose is to love and be loved by him. But he also gives us a mission to accomplish. We may not be called to lead an army like Gideon, but we may be asked to embark on a particular career, to raise a family, or to accomplish great things through prayer. Inevitably, we will face times in which we simply do not feel up to the task. We will not want to face one more cranky child, one more day on a stressful job, one more person who needs our prayers.

When that happens, it might be worth thinking about Gideon and the angel that called his name. Gideon knew he had none of the right credentials for saving Israel. As he pointed out to the angel, he was the low man on the totem pole. That may even have been why the angel called his name. God wanted there to be no mistake about who would deserve the credit for saving Israel. A stronger man than Gideon might have demanded the glory for himself.

At one point, Gideon had rallied thirty-two thousand men to fight with him against the Midianites. But God told him, in effect, "You have too many men for me to deliver the Midianites into their hands. Israel would only take the credit away from me, saying, 'My own hand has delivered me.'" So God pared them back to a mere three hundred men, less than 1 percent of the original army! The reason Gideon succeeded was not because of who he was, but because of who was on his side.

If you feel that you do not have the right credentials to do what God has asked of you, you are probably right. But if God has called your name, he will be with you. He may even send an angel to give you a vision for who you really are: a mighty warrior determined to do God's will, to take great risks, and to make the necessary sacrifices in his service.

Lord, you know how weak I really am. I ask you to make my weakness raw material for your grace. Your power is made perfect in weakness such as mine. Thank you that you choose the foolish things of this world to confound the wise. Do great things in me, and then take your glory, Lord.

A DREAM OF ANGELS

✍

Mary had been engaged to Joseph, but before they lived together, she was found to be with child from the Holy Spirit. Her husband Joseph, being a righteous man and unwilling to expose her to public disgrace, planned to dismiss her quietly. But just when he had resolved to do this, an angel of the Lord appeared to him in a dream.

Matthew 1:18–20 NRSV

The angels played a major role in all the events surrounding Jesus' birth, not the least of which was their role as messengers to Joseph. Three times this man saw angels in his dreams. The first time was to convince him that the impossible had happened: Mary was pregnant though she had not been unfaithful to him. Next an angel warned Joseph to take his family and flee to Egypt, where they would be safe from Herod's wrath. And on the last occasion Joseph was told to return to the land of Israel after Herod had died.

We don't know a great deal about Joseph, but we do know that he must have been a man willing to take the risks that faith required. As a young man Joseph must have had dreams for himself. His engagement to Mary may have marked the beginning of a way of life he intended to live: to work hard, prosper, and raise a family in Nazareth, as his father before him had done. But his plans were disrupted by angels. He would flee Bethlehem with Mary and the infant in the middle of the night, escaping to a foreign land to elude the wrath of a power-mad king. It would be several years before he would see Nazareth again.

Of course Joseph had a choice in the matter each time the angels appeared to him. The first time he could have brushed the angel off as nothing more than a product of his own wishful thinking. When in the long history of the world had a woman ever become pregnant without sleeping with a man? He could have set Mary aside as he had planned to do and married someone else. But Joseph heeded the angel and said yes to God's plan for his life.

Did Joseph comprehend the enormity of the decision he was making? Possibly, he did. But certainly, he could not foresee the strange mixture of blessing and suffering that lay in store for him and his family. His yes would cost him many sleepless nights, but it would also involve him in the greatest miracle of all time.

God has a dream for each one of us, and sometimes that dream interrupts the dream we have for our own lives. Like Joseph, we have a choice to make. We can reject the dream and move on with our life as planned. Or we can welcome the dream, even though we don't understand all the implications. If we say yes to God, we will encounter an adventure that will involve both agony and joy. In the end, it will have been well worth the risk. Ultimately, the choice is always ours.

My Father, help me to let go of lesser dreams, that I might fully grasp hold of every good thing you have for me. Let there not come a time when I let my yes become a maybe and my maybe become a no. Give me the courage to follow wherever you lead. Help me to dream the dreams you have for me.

PART 2

MIRACULOUS ENCOUNTERS

A WORD ABOUT MIRACLES

Imagine for a moment that one of your children is in danger. She is walking blindfolded toward the edge of a cliff. A few more steps and she will tumble to her death. You are standing a football field away. What do you do? Fortunately, you happen to have a megaphone in your hand. You shout through it, imploring her to stop and turn around before it's too late.

This is one way of understanding why God performs miracles. At times, they are his megaphone to children who have wandered into dangerous territory and to a world that has grown deaf to the divine voice. But miracles often happen to people who live close to God as well. Perhaps it is enough to say that miracles appear to be an extraordinary form of divine communication. They capture our attention in compelling ways.

Signs and wonders, the biblical terms for miracles, always convey some kind of spiritual message. And, as in any conversation, the message varies, depending on the circumstances in which it is delivered. Sometimes a miracle reveals God's power, sometimes his mercy or his graciousness. Always, such wonders are a sign of the in-breaking of the divine kingdom, a down payment on our future with God.

I hope the stories that follow, both from Scripture and from ordinary men and women, will nourish your faith that God is still in control of our chaotic world. It is my conviction that the same God who met Moses in the desert and spoke to him from the midst of a fiery bush longs to speak to us today — to tell us of his tender love, his power, and his desire to deliver us from harm. Whether you are standing at a cliff's edge or sitting in a comfortable chair in your living room, I hope these stories will draw you closer to the only One who can be your refuge in every kind of trouble.

12

MIRACLES HAPPEN WHEN YOU PRAY

Prayer enlarges the heart until it is capable of containing God's gift of Himself. Ask and seek and your heart will grow big enough to receive Him and keep Him as your own.

Mother Teresa of Calcutta

When faced with a dilemma or personal tragedy too large for any human being to handle, I have sometimes thrown up my hands and said: "All I can do is pray." Over the years, I have come to realize how ridiculous such a statement really is. It's as though I were to become frustrated with a piggy bank I couldn't open and to say: "Well, all I can do is light this stick of dynamite and hope that it blows things apart." That's what prayer is like—a spiritual explosive with the power to reconfigure the natural world.

That doesn't mean that every prayer we utter will result in a miracle. Despite our longings, a miracle may be the last thing we need. But it does mean that our requests are heard by the highest authority in the universe, by the only one both powerful enough and wise enough to answer our prayers effectively.

Like anything else, prayer takes practice. To learn to pray is to learn at least two basic lessons: surrender and persistence.

What exactly does it mean to *surrender* in prayer? Most often, we pray with definite ideas in mind. We think a problem will only be solved if God does this or that and does it right now. But the anxiety we bring to prayer can quickly transform our intercession into nothing more than an attempt to manipulate God. The first step, then, is to ask for grace to let go of our desire to control both the method and the outcome. As we do this, we will find our anxiety ebbing and a new peace taking hold as the Spirit reshapes our prayer according to God's will.

Besides surrender, we need to learn *persistence*. One of the greatest enemies of prayer is discouragement. We become disheartened because we pray and nothing seems to happen. Worse yet, the situation we are praying for deteriorates. Jesus himself spoke of the necessity of persistence when he encouraged his followers to keep asking God for what they needed. Persistence is, in fact, the yeast of prayer.

You may be thinking right now of an urgent prayer. Perhaps you have been praying this prayer for some time. Try to quiet yourself in the presence of God. Ask him to deal with your anxiety and show you how to pray so that you might take your place next to Jesus, who is always interceding at the Father's right hand.

THE WEDDING MIRACLE

When the wine was gone, Jesus' mother said to him, "They have no more wine." "Dear woman, why do you involve me?" Jesus replied. "My time has not yet come." His mother said to the servants, "Do whatever he tells you."

John 2:3–5

I f anyone ever had perfect timing it was Jesus. He never missed a beat. In tune with his Father's will, he would only embark on his public ministry when God gave the go-ahead, not before. So why does he seem to change his mind so quickly? Why does he perform a miracle that started tongues wagging all over Galilee?

Somehow Jesus must have known that Mary's prayer had changed things, suddenly setting his public ministry in motion. His hidden life had come to an end. Now the light of the world would reveal itself, a counterpoint against the darkness.

Jesus wastes no time, ordering the servants at the wedding feast described in John's gospel to take six stone water jars, the kind the Jews used for ceremonial cleansing, and fill them with water. Then he tells them to call the steward so that he can draw out its contents and taste it. As soon as it passes his lips, the man recognizes it as the most exquisite wine he has ever tasted, and he cannot imagine why the bride and groom have withheld the best wine until last.

As usual, the miracle is about more than a simple wedding feast in Cana. It is about transforming the ordinary into the extraordinary, the natural into the supernatural, the kingdom of this world into the kingdom of God, law into grace, and death into life. It is about the blood of a Savior whose body would be broken on a tree, so that from it would flow streams of living water. It is about a wedding feast in heaven to be celebrated at the end of time. It is about mercy, joy, and communion—and about the passionate love of God for his people.

Remarkably, this wonderful miracle came about because Mary noticed someone else's need and brought it to her son's attention. Because of the simple prayer of a compassionate woman, grace was released that set the saving plan of God in motion. It may even be that the Father was waiting for a prayer like hers before shifting things into high gear. Whatever the case, we should be encouraged. This miracle urges us to pray. For we are not merely members of the audience, passively entertained by the drama of salvation. Our prayers actually help to set the stage and may even raise the curtain on the next act of God's work in the history of the world.

Lord, it amazes me that your power accomplishes so many things at once. With this miracle, you encouraged us to pray, you showed compassion to a poor family, you began your reign, and you gave your people a glimpse of your plan of salvation. I am astonished by the wonderful efficiency of your grace. Help me to recognize the needs of others and then to call them calmly and confidently to your attention. Like Mary, let me trust you to answer my prayers as you see fit.

LOST AND FOUND

Again, I tell you that if two of you on earth agree about anything you ask for, it will be done for you by my Father in heaven. For where two or three come together in my name, there am I with them.

Matthew 18:19–20

Alan Smith and his wife, Leisa, had spent part of the day raking leaves and pine straw from his mother-in-law's backyard. His young daughter, Lydia, was helping grandma too, in typical four-year-old fashion. They worked hard through the afternoon and as twilight edged across the horizon, they straightened their backs, stretched, and looked with satisfaction on their handiwork.

The yard looked great. Huge pine trees shimmered green against the deepening blue sky. Beautiful as they were, these same trees had made a mess of the yard, yielding twelve bags full of pine straw. Now the black lawn bags were piled together in the middle of the grass.

Their sense of satisfaction was cut short as Leisa suddenly exclaimed, "Oh, no! My ring is gone. It could be anywhere on the lawn or in one of those bags." Her diamond engagement ring had slipped off her finger as she worked.

"We all felt sick, but I decided we could do something about it," explained Alan. "So I said, 'Let's just pray right now. God knows where it is.' We sat down on the grass and asked him to show one of us where the ring was. We closed our eyes and just stayed quiet for a minute. Suddenly, my four-year-old jumped up and said, 'I know where it is!' She walked over to all those bags of pine straw and pulled one out. It wasn't the first one or the one on the edge either. Lydia went to one in the middle of all the bags and said, 'Open this one.' We didn't even have to dump out the contents. As soon as I opened it and spilled a little of the straw, out came the ring!"

What a wonderful experience for this small family! To pray together for their need and to see God use the tiniest member to perform a miracle. That day the Smith family rejoiced, not just because something of value was restored to them but because something precious was added to their faith.

Lord, you tell us that only those who become like little children will enter your kingdom. Give me the simple humility and faith of a child as I seek you for the desires closest to my heart. Then help me to follow your leading as you answer my prayers.

THE PRAYER OF A CHILD

Which of you, if his son asks for bread, will give him a stone? Or if he asks for a fish, will give him a snake? If you, then, though you are evil, know how to give good gifts to your children, how much more will your Father in heaven give good gifts to those who ask him!

Matthew 7:9–11

Most small children would choose a candy bar over an apple any day. But Andrew Weigand wasn't just any three-and-a-half-year-old. This boy had never tasted the tartness of an apple or savored the sound of one snapping crisply between his teeth. For that matter, he never ate pears, oranges, plums, grapes, cherries, strawberries, blueberries, raspberries, watermelon, peaches, apricots, nectarines, or any other kind of fruit under the sun except bananas. Since infancy, Andrew had suffered from severe food allergies that would cause him to pay for the slightest mistake with a blistery rash and a bad case of diarrhea. As a baby, he would scream every time he wet his diaper.

To make matters worse, Andrew attended a toddler's group in church that was forever singing a cheery little song that went like this: "Who can make an apple? I'm sure I can't. Can you? Oh, who can make an apple? Only God can. It is true." Then each of the kids would be given a piece of fake fruit and the adults would talk about how fruit is good for you, how God wants kids to have the fruit of the Spirit, and how God gives fruit to make us healthy. More than anything, Andrew wanted to be able to eat an apple like the other kids. His mother, Marie, could see the conflict playing out in his young mind. "We can pray, Andrew," she told him. "That's all we can do. Mommy doesn't have a medicine that will take care of the problem, but Jesus might heal you if we ask him."

One day she decided to take her son to a healing service at a local church. At one point the man who was leading the prayer service said he believed God was healing someone of severe food allergies. "My heart jumped," said Marie. "I placed my hand on Andrew's head and asked God to deal with the allergies. But I still wasn't sure anything had happened, so I decided to take him up front for more prayer. During the entire service, I experienced a tremendous sense of peace, but I really didn't know whether my son had been healed.

"All the way home a friend who was with us kept repeating, 'Andrew, you're healed! You're going to go home and eat an apple.' Her certainty irritated me, and I kept hushing her because I didn't want to get Andrew's hopes up. But it was too late.

"When I suggested he start with a small slice of apple, Andrew looked at me and said, 'You know I'm healed. I don't know why you're not giving me the whole thing.' I was reluctant to trust the faith of a toddler, but my husband encouraged me to give it a try so I did. I braced myself for the inevitable, but nothing happened, not the slightest rash, no diarrhea, nothing. A few months earlier, a one-inch cube of watermelon was enough to set off a violent reaction. But that day Andrew ate the apple like any other healthy kid. Now he eats grapes like crazy and spreads cherry jam on his bagel. He has had absolutely no problems with any kind of food allergy.

"I really don't know why God healed Andrew when so many people suffer from much more serious problems, but I do know that this is one mother and son who never doubt that our God is a God of love and mercy."

Father, you know how hard it is for us to see our children suffer. We feel so helpless and frustrated by their pain. When this happens, help us to remember that we are utterly dependent on you just as our children are dependent on us. May we come to you with a child's confidence that you are who you say you are—a loving and all-powerful Father, one who pays attention to our prayers and answers them with both wisdom and mercy.

A MIRACLE OF
SHEER PERSISTENCE

"That you may know that the Son of Man has authority on earth to forgive sins...." He said to the paralytic, "I tell you, get up, take your mat and go home." He got up, took his mat and walked out in full view of them all.

Mark 2:10 – 12

A crowd had gathered on the edge of the shores of Galilee. People were jammed into the house in Capernaum where Jesus was preaching, anxious to catch sight of the man who had cast out demons and even cured a leper. Many Pharisees were there as well. Believers and skeptics filled the room. People spilled out the doorway, like too many beans in a jar. Everyone wanted to hear what the rabbi was saying inside.

Four men approached, carrying a man who was paralyzed. They too had heard the wonderful stories about Jesus. Perhaps he would do something for their friend whose limbs looked like spindly branches strewn carelessly across the mat on which he lay. But so thick was the crowd that they couldn't push through. Undeterred, the men lifted their friend to the roof and began to remove the tile and thatch that covered it. As they worked, they could hear the voice of Jesus below.

At first the crowd seemed oblivious to what was happening. Suddenly, Jesus stopped speaking. All eyes were fixed on the paralytic as he made his slow descent from the ceiling. Delighted by the faith of the men who had lowered him through the roof, Jesus said to the paralytic: "Son, your sins are forgiven."

His words astonished the Pharisees. They knew the law and the law said that God alone could forgive sins.

"This man is a fraud. He is blaspheming God!"

Instantly, Jesus discerned their unspoken thoughts and said to them, "Why are you thinking these things? Which is easier: to say to the paralytic, 'Your sins are forgiven,' or to say, 'Get up, take your mat and walk'? But that you may know that the Son of Man has authority on earth to forgive sins...." Jesus then looked at the paralytic and said, "I tell you, get up, take your mat and go home" (Mark 2:8–11).

The paralytic man got up, picked up his mat, and walked out of the house in full view of everyone there. All the people in the house were amazed, and they praised God with these words, "We have never seen anything like this!" (Mark 2:12).

Anyone could have spoken a word of false comfort to the paralyzed man, telling him his sins were forgiven, but only God had the power to enable him to get off his mat and walk out the door. Clearly, this Jesus had power over the soul as well as the body. The Pharisees needed a tangible sign that Jesus could forgive sins. Perhaps the paralytic himself needed proof that his sins were forgiven. How could he doubt it now? His arms and legs were straight, his mat was in his hand, and he was striding away from the house a new man.

The people had seen the invalid's atrophied limbs. But Jesus had seen his atrophied soul. So he dealt with what was inside the man before touching and restoring what was on the outside.

So often, we come to God asking for a miracle: to cure a sick friend, bring back a wayward child, heal an eating disorder, save a troubled marriage. We think we know what will make us happy. But God always penetrates the surface of our need to deal with the core problem. He is not interested in performing miracles that only display his power. He wants to perform miracles that reveal his love. And so he deals, not just with our pain, but with the source of our pain; not just with the infirmity of our bodies, but with the infirmity of our hearts. Like the paralytic's friends, we are called to pray with faith. As we do, God will forgive our sins and then touch us with his power.

Father, sometimes it is easier for me to believe in your power than in your mercy. Help me to be quick to surrender my sins to your mercy, rather than stubbornly standing in judgment of myself. Give me the assurance, as you did the man paralyzed by sin, that you really have forgiven me. Finally, grant me the same persistent love and bold faith of the men who lowered their brother, the paralytic, into the presence of Jesus. Then let me trust him for the results.

THE MIRACLE OF PERSISTENT LOVE

⤬

I have heard your prayer and seen your tears; I will heal you.

2 Kings 20:5

Bob Mardock was associate pastor at the Eugene Friends Church in Eugene, Oregon, when it happened. He and other members of his church conducted a prayer service every Tuesday. Anyone who wanted could come for extended times of prayer, often lasting for two or three hours for one person. They called it "soaking prayer."

"One day, a woman I'll call Jean came in for prayer. She was a tough case. Diagnosed with lupus, her hair was falling out, her face was bloated, her skin was scaly, and she looked really awful. But we said we would pray and so we did. Actually, we prayed for her every week for six months.

"During that time, she began to tell us many things about her past that we were able to pray through. As a young woman she had been the victim of incest and had suffered all kinds of physical and emotional abuse. Hooked on drugs, she had eventually gotten pregnant. Her life was a mess, but we kept praying. Gradually, she got better. Her skin cleared up, her hair started to grow back, and she felt great. This woman was verging on death when we first met her. After six months of prayer, we saw her life transformed like a living miracle. Not only was her body healthy but her soul was restored. Years of sin and abuse had been surrendered to God and healed.

"I stayed in touch with Jean for a few years. As it turned out, she was especially gifted in praying for others. At one point, she was hired to head up the prayer ministry at a church in Washington. I can't offer you proof positive that the lupus never returned, though I have no reason to think it did. Whatever the case, I am absolutely certain that God performed a miracle in her life through prayer."

Jean's story reminds us that God wants to heal our souls as well as our bodies. How easy it would be for him to simply wave his almighty hand and command our symptoms to disappear. For many of us, that's all we really want. We'd rather not dig too deeply to expose our deepest problems. But fortunately, God is never content to merely treat our symptoms. Instead, he prescribes a remedy that is often administered through the loving hands and hearts of ordinary people, friends who will not let us go no matter how hard and long the road to healing may be.

Father, it's your love that heals us, body and soul. Thank you for the way you reveal this tremendous love through other people. Help me to realize that persistent prayer is nothing other than persistent love. May I remember this when I am tempted to quit praying. As I persist, reveal your love through me.

13

MIRACLES OF HEALING

❧

*I believe in miraculous cures, and I shall never forget
the impact I felt watching with my own eyes how an enormous
cancerous growth on the hand of a worker dissolved
and changed into a light scar. I cannot understand, but I
can even less doubt what I saw with my own eyes.*

Dr. Alexis Carrel, Nobel Prize in Medicine, 1913

It was no surprise that my request for miracle stories generated more descriptions of physical healing than any other kind of miracle. As creatures in a fallen world, we often feel our separation from paradise most acutely in our bodies. Illness, in fact, is often a precursor of death and is, itself, a smaller kind of death. Interestingly, Paul's letter to the Romans traces the root of our problem: it tells us that "the wages of sin is death" (Romans 6:23).

As Louis Mondon, the author of *Signs and Wonders*, has pointed out, the flesh is the "theatre of the redemptive work." So it makes sense that God would sometimes heal our bodies as a way of revealing his mercy and saving grace.

In fact, when God touches our flesh it is to impart a deeper message to our spirits. Ultimately, this is what gives lasting significance to such miracles. Otherwise, every miracle of healing performed on mortal creatures would eventually be undone.

As Monden points out, miracles of healing have more in common with Christ's transfiguration on the mountaintop than with his resurrection. There the veil was lifted for a moment to reveal Jesus' glory to his disciples. But the decisive victory had not yet been won. Jesus still had to face Gethsemane and Golgotha. So too we still face suffering and sorrow and many trials in the years that are left to us. To echo the familiar words of the poet Robert Frost, we yet have many "miles to go before we sleep."

If you or someone you love is suffering from some kind of physical or mental disorder, I hope you will take heart from the stories that follow. Who knows whether God will stretch out his hand and touch you with a miracle? But whether or not he does, never stop clinging to him. For one day "he will wipe every tear from [your] eyes. There will be no more death or mourning or crying or pain, for the old order of things has passed away" (Revelation 21:4).

AN ENEMY HEALED

When Jesus' followers saw what was going to happen, they said, "Lord, should we strike with our swords?" And one of them struck the servant of the high priest, cutting off his right ear. But Jesus answered, "No more of this!" And he touched the man's ear and healed him.

Luke 22:49–51

A few years ago, I had the opportunity of visiting Israel with a small group of friends. One day we were traveling through a region northeast of Tel Aviv when we passed through the valley of Armageddon, the place where the book of Revelation pinpoints the world's last battle. As our small bus traveled past this foreboding place, I noticed one of my fellow passengers asleep across the aisle. Later, we joked that Bill was the only person we knew who had actually slept through Armageddon.

Centuries earlier, Jesus' disciples managed to sleep through one of the darkest moments in salvation history. After the Passover meal they followed him to the Mount of Olives. As Jesus agonized in prayer about his coming suffering, his followers dozed off. But as soon as they awoke, they found themselves faced with a detachment of soldiers and officials from the chief priests and Pharisees, intent on arresting their master.

Taken by surprise, they asked Jesus whether they should draw their swords against the crowd. Without waiting for his reply, Peter cut off the ear of Malchus, servant to the high priest. But Jesus rebuked Peter, picked up the man's ear, and proceeded to fasten it in place as though it had never been torn from his head.

I wonder who was more surprised: Malchus or Peter? Why would a man with this kind of power use it to heal his enemy? Why would he allow himself to be arrested in the first place? It was too much for Peter and the disciples, who promptly abandoned Jesus to his fate.

With the benefit of hindsight, we recognize how foolish Peter was. But as usual, this impetuous follower of Christ acts as a mirror reflecting our own behavior. How do we respond when the gospel comes under attack—in the media, in our schools, in our neighborhoods, or in the political arena? What happens when we come under some kind of personal attack? Do we fortify ourselves with prayer, asking for grace to know and be faithful to the divine strategy as Jesus did in Gethsemane? Or have we too fallen asleep in the hour of darkness?

Once we awaken to the threat, do we respond like Peter, thinking that Jesus is too weak to defend himself? If so, we may resort to dirty tricks and name-calling, demonizing anyone who opposes us. In our fear, we may circle the wagons and reduce the gospel of Christ to mere politics.

But the lesson of Gethsemane is that we must join Jesus as he prays to the Father for the strength to do his will. Only then will we be given the necessary grace to respond in faith rather than fear, in courage rather than self-defensiveness.

Lord, I thank you that Peter was far from perfect. His mistakes somehow manage to encourage me. Even though he was one of your closest friends and followers, he often misunder-

stood you and entirely missed the point. But still you were patient with him, and his faith grew strong in the process. Help me to learn from my mistakes, and teach me how to pray in your presence.

HEALING PRESENCE

Therefore my heart is glad and my tongue rejoices;
my body also will rest secure,
because you will not abandon me to the grave,
nor will you let your Holy One see decay.
You have made known to me the path of life;
you will fill me with joy in your presence,
with eternal pleasures at your right hand.

Psalm 16:9–11

In her book *Meeting God at Every Turn*, Catherine Marshall tells a remarkable story about her struggle with tuberculosis. Diagnosed in 1943 at Johns Hopkins in Baltimore, she was devastated to hear the news that she would need three to four months of complete bed rest. She could only get up to use the bathroom. How could she possibly confine her world to a sickbed when her three-year-old son needed her? Little did she know those few months would stretch into two frustrating years as each visit to the doctor revealed absolutely no improvement.

Fortunately, her enforced rest was anything but wasted. Catherine spent her time reading Scripture and exploring God's character, asking him the hard questions of faith and probing beneath the surface for the answers she sought. Not surprisingly, one of her questions had to do with whether God still healed people. As a child she had learned that miracles had ceased with the early church. Yet page after page of the Gospels revealed a Jesus who loved to heal people. So eager was he to touch the sick, blind, and lame with his healing power that he couldn't wait even twenty-four hours to avoid performing a miracle on the Sabbath—a practice that deeply offended the religious leaders of his day. How could this same Jesus refrain from healing people for two thousand years? She didn't believe he could or would. So she and her husband, Peter, prayed fervently for a miracle. But none came.

Still, they continued to pray. Finally, after many days of internal struggle, Catherine uttered an honest prayer of complete abandonment, telling God he could do whatever he wanted with her. She would accept his will even if it meant she would be an invalid for the rest of her life. He didn't have to explain himself to her, because she trusted him to love and provide for her no matter what happened. That prayer was a turning point. The same night, while staying with her parents, she had an experience that changed her life:

"In the middle of that night I was awakened. The room was in total darkness. Instantly sensing something alive, electric in the room, I sat bolt upright in bed. Past all credible belief, suddenly, unaccountably, Christ was there, in Person, standing by the right side of my bed. I could see nothing but a deep, velvety blackness around me, but the bedroom was filled with an intensity of power, as if the Dynamo of the universe were there. Every nerve in my body tingled with it, as with a shock of electricity. I knew that Jesus was smiling at me tenderly, lovingly, whimsically—as though a trifle amused at my too-intense seriousness about myself. His attitude seemed to say, 'Relax! There's not a thing wrong here that I can't take care of.'"

Then she heard a voice instruct her to "go and tell her mother." This puzzled and frightened her. It was after all, the middle of the night. What was she supposed to say to her mother? Would her mother think she had lost her senses?

Still, she had the feeling that her future depended on her obedience. "I groped my way into the dark hall to the bedroom directly across from mine and spoke softly to Mother and Dad. Startled, Mother sat bolt upright in bed. 'Catherine, is anything wrong? What — what on earth has happened?'

" 'It's all right,' I reassured them. 'I just want to tell you that I'll be all right now. It seemed important to tell you tonight. I'll give you the details tomorrow.' "

Soon after, X-rays showed a marked improvement in Catherine's condition. The long siege was drawing to a close. Within six months, the doctors pronounced her completely well.

So often it seems we can only learn the lessons of faith the hard way — by wrestling with God in the midst of whatever darkness he allows in our lives. But if we wrestle as Catherine Marshall did, with a determination to know God better, we will one day enjoy a deeper sense of his presence. We may even sense that he's smiling at us, telling us to relax in the knowledge that there's not a thing wrong that he can't take care of.

Lord, I'm a fighter by nature. "Never give up" is my life motto. If one thing won't work, then I'll try another and another and another. Help me to realize when it's time to fight and when it's time to surrender. You know the areas in my life that require surrender. Right now, I ask for the help to relinquish these to you. Give me the grace to say yes to your will. Not a yes spoken through gritted teeth, but an honest yes, spoken in a quiet place in my soul, the place where you dwell.

A Miracle of the Mind

Then Jesus said to his disciples, "If anyone would come after me, he must deny himself and take up his cross and follow me. For whoever wants to save his life will lose it, but whoever loses his life for me will find it."

Matthew 16:24–25

Philip Luebbert had a lot going for him. Raised in a loving family, he excelled in school, and even made the dean's list in college. Eventually he enrolled in a seminary in St. Paul, Minnesota, to fulfill his childhood dream of becoming a priest. But by the time Philip was twenty-one, his dream was shattered. Though he didn't know it then, his mind was being overtaken by a terrible disorder. Philip was suffering from schizophrenia.

"Unless you have lived through it, you cannot possibly imagine the horror that fills your mind—the terror that distorts your view of the world. You have emotions that most people will never experience," Philip explains. "I would be in a baseball stadium, for instance, and would be convinced that everybody was staring at me. Thousands of eyes just looking at Phil Luebbert. I became obsessed with religion, convinced that God was punishing me. And no matter what anyone said to me, I refused to get help.

"It got so bad that one day, when I was twenty-three, I simply lost it. I got into my car and started driving. I drove as fast as I could, straight for a bridge embankment. But suddenly, and I really don't know how this happened, I felt compelled to put my foot on the brake. It was as though some kind of irresistible force inside me made me switch my foot from the gas to the brakes. I crashed into the embankment but at a much slower speed. The car was totaled, but I walked away from the wreck — and straight into a mental hospital. From there it seemed like an endless stream of hospitals and doctors, and all of them said the same thing. Philip Luebbert would never hold down a job. He would never be able to live on his own. He would never have much of a life.

"I couldn't stop asking God, 'Why me? What did I ever do to deserve this? All I ever wanted was to live for you and serve you.' I felt so betrayed. But despite my questions, I couldn't rid myself of the notion that God was, after all, a loving God who was powerful enough to heal me. Deep down, I knew he wouldn't abandon me, and I continued to pray regularly and ask his forgiveness whenever I felt I offended him. The church was a haven for me throughout this time. Despite my confusion, I just couldn't give up on God — and he didn't give up on me.

"My healing didn't happen overnight. But gradually I began to improve, and in 1987 I landed my first job — as a dishwasher. It wasn't the job I dreamed of as a young man, but after what I had been through, it was astonishing that I could work at all. I thought my folks would explode with joy when I told them the news. My life will never be what I thought it would be as a young boy. I know the ravages of the disease still linger to some degree. But anyone who knew me during the years of my hospitalization would tell you that a tremendous miracle of healing has occurred in my life.

"I still don't know why I have had to struggle with this disease. But through it I have come to love the cross of Christ. I now know without a doubt that suffering can be redemptive. When I didn't know what to do, when there was no place to go for help, when I was on the verge of despair, I just kept clinging to God. And he was there. He saved me. He restored me. And he has a purpose for my life."

Father, each of us has a cross to bear in this life—some sorrow or suffering that shapes our souls for better or worse. Whatever it may be, help us to take courage from the cross of your Son. May we hold fast to you no matter what. And as we cling to you, mold us with your loving hands and shape us into your likeness.

One Miracle at a Time

He lifted me out of the slimy pit,
*   out of the mud and mire;*
he set my feet on a rock
*   and gave me a firm place to stand.*
He put a new song in my mouth,
*   a hymn of praise to our God.*

Psalm 40:2–3

Carlene Miller's livelihood depended on her voice. She was on the phone constantly negotiating lease agreements with other companies. In 1993 she came down with what she thought was a bad case of laryngitis. But it was worse than that. A specialist told her she was suffering from a paralyzed vocal chord, probably as a result of a virus. Time would tell whether it would heal or whether her voice would be reduced to a whisper for the rest of her life. There was nothing the specialist could do.

The thought was intolerable to Carlene, who also enjoyed a singing ministry in local churches. Now she could neither sing nor talk in a normal voice. After three or four words, she would have to pause for breath. At work, she wrote scripts for her secretary, hoping to get by until her voice returned. But it just wasn't working.

Still, the specialist told her that her chances of recovery were good, though it would take at least six months. It had already been five weeks, and Carlene wondered if she could stand another day of it. To make matters worse, she had recently been diagnosed with chronic fatigue syndrome. She worried that she might lose her job.

"I was so crushed by the news," she said, "that I went home and cried on my roommate, Lori's, shoulder. Later, I got a call from someone at church inviting me to attend the weekly worship team practice the next evening. Even though I couldn't sing a note, I agreed to go because my friends there wanted to pray for me.

"But I had to work late the next day and was exhausted as a result of my chronic fatigue. All I could think of was how much I wanted to lie down. If I could just get some sleep. But Lori, who isn't particularly religious, insisted I go to church. 'Normally, I would tell you to stay home,' she said, 'but the people in your church want to pray for you, and I think you should go. I'll even drive you.'

"So we went and Lori sat in the back watching as the choir surrounded me to pray for my healing. They prayed out loud and then began singing. After about twenty minutes of this, some of the members began playing instruments. It turned into an impromptu worship fest, and the music was so beautiful that I almost forgot why I was there. The presence of God was so palpable I began to cry.

"Suddenly I had this strange notion that I should open my mouth and shout at the top of my lungs. It seemed ridiculous. How could I shout when talking was so painful? I had hardly been able to whisper for five weeks. But the thought kept getting stronger until I couldn't stand it anymore. So I just yelled, 'It's back!' and then everyone started to cry. Somehow God gave me the faith to shout that my voice was healed before I even knew it.

"On the way home, Lori kept saying, 'If I hadn't driven you here and heard you try to talk for the past several weeks, I wouldn't have believed it.'

"After that, my voice was strong as ever, except that I lost some range in my singing, which returned after a few months' practice. I was so overjoyed and full of faith that I just knew I would wake up the next morning without even a symptom of my chronic fatigue. The God I worshiped was a God of miracles. But I awoke feeling more tired than ever. The chronic fatigue was there in full force. I wondered why God would heal my voice but not the rest of me. It would be a while before I began to comprehend his reasons. But now I knew without a doubt that God cared about what was happening to me and that he was in control of my life."

Lord, you are a God who hears even our inaudible cries, a loving King who inhabits the praises of his people. As we come into your healing presence, let the music of our voices blend to form a refrain of praise that you will find beautiful to listen to.

"A Dream
Healed My Fear"

The Lord is with me; I will not be afraid.

Psalm 118:6

Debby, a mother of three children, records the following story. "I have sometimes wondered whether I might lose my faith if something really terrible happened. That fear must have been lurking in the background when I had a horrible nightmare three years ago, in the early morning hours of Labor Day (1993).

"For as long as I can remember I have had a problem with claustrophobia. It especially bothers me if my legs are constricted in any way. The thought that I might not be able to move them is enough to drive me crazy.

"In my dream I am trapped in an underground tunnel. I am alone in the darkness, and I can hardly breathe. I have no idea how I got there or what has happened. I only know I am buried alive. I cannot move my legs. I am suffocating. I am so terrified that I wake up.

"Afterward, I felt such a sense of panic that I had to get out of bed and walk around, reassuring myself it had not really happened.

"Whenever dreams leave such a strong impression, I have found it good to pray about them in case God is trying to tell me something. That morning I asked myself how I would react if I really were buried alive. Would God still be with me? Would I lose my faith? I didn't know the answer.

"As I was praying and turning these things over in my mind, it suddenly occurred to me to wonder about the circumstances of my birth. My mother had always told me it had been a breech birth. I assumed that meant I had entered the world bottom first. Perhaps my claustrophobia was connected to this early trauma. As I continued to pray, I felt God reassuring me. Just as he had brought me safely through the birth canal, he would bring me safely through life. Whatever difficulty I faced, he would be there. I didn't think I was imagining the message of his comfort.

"Two days later the strangest thing happened. My mother and I were talking on the phone when she brought up the subject of my birth. She had been out walking the dog on Labor Day when a thought popped into her head: 'I wonder if Debbie knows about her breech birth.' I told her I knew that a breech birth meant the baby came out bottom first. 'Not in your case,' she told me. 'You came out with your legs straight in front of you.'

"No wonder I was so sensitive whenever my legs felt constricted! It all fell into place. The dream, God's reassurance, my mother's revelation. By praying through the dream and talking to my mother, I had been given a deeper understanding of God's care. I couldn't help but chuckle at God's timing. I knew it was no accident that he began showing me the connection between my fear and the circumstances of my birth on the very day we celebrate as Labor Day."

Lord, you know me even better than I know myself. You were there at the beginning and you will be with me until the end. Help me to rest in this assurance.

14

MIRACLES THAT MULTIPLY

Miracles do not happen in contradiction of nature,
but in contradiction of what we know about nature.

Saint Augustine

Even in an affluent society, so many of our problems seem to stem from scarcity. We feel we have too little money, too little time, too little love and patience. No matter how much money we set aside, we still worry about the future. Will inflation erode our nest egg? Will college costs keep soaring? How will we possibly find the time and energy to care for aging parents? Somehow, there is not enough of us, or the things we need, to go around. We are finite creatures with infinite aspirations.

When I am feeling this way, I like to recall the miracles of multiplication that God has already performed. As always, there is more to these miracles than meets the eye. When Jesus breaks the bread and it is multiplied, he offers us a glimpse of himself as the bread of life. When the disciples enjoy a record catch of fish, we realize they are to become fishers of souls. Scratch the surface of a miracle and you will find layers of spiritual meaning. Reduce the miraculous merely to its literal meaning and you will miss the point entirely.

So the next time you feel spiritually hungry, remind Jesus that he is, after all, the bread of life. The next time you run up against your limitations, use them as an opportunity to become more dependent on him. Be honest about your spiritual emptiness. Wrestle with Jesus' words, his promises, and his wonders until your soul finds the nourishment it craves. Give God what little you have—of faith, of desire, of perseverance—and ask him to multiply it a hundredfold.

AN EDUCATION
IN MIRACLES

Taking the five loaves and the two fish and looking up to heaven, [Jesus] gave thanks and broke the loaves. Then he gave them to the disciples and the disciples gave them to the people. They all ate and were satisfied, and the disciples picked up twelve basketfuls of broken pieces that were left over.

Matthew 14:19–20

You remember the story. Jesus and his disciples had just heard the news of John the Baptist's beheading. Now they sought a quiet place to make sense of this new sorrow. But the clamoring crowd followed and met them on the shore as they crossed the Sea of Galilee. As the boat drew near, Jesus could see them and hear their exultant shouts:

"I see him!"

"There he is, the miracle worker!"

"The one that drives out devils and even raises the dead!"

There were so many of them: the sick in soul, the lepers, the blind, the lame, the prostitutes and beggars. Each one had a hope, each a need. He knew their stories without asking.

He had been longing for rest, but his heart was stirred with compassion for the men and women thronging the shore. He spent the day moving among them, teaching them and healing the sick.

But as evening approached, his disciples began to worry. What would happen when the sun went down? They were in a remote place with nothing to feed the crowd, which by now had swollen to several thousand people. Eight months' wages wouldn't be enough to feed a group this large.

So they did what you and I probably would have done. They suggested the obvious: Jesus should disperse the crowd so that each man could find food for his family in the surrounding villages. But Jesus astonished them with his reply: "How many loaves do you have?" They must have wondered why he would even ask such a crazy question. It would be like asking how many hot dogs you had in your sack lunch to feed the fans in Yankee Stadium. "Five *small* loaves and two *small* fish," was their answer, as if to emphasize how little they had to meet such an enormous need.

Then Jesus asked the disciples to get the people to sit down in groups on the grass, and he proceeded to give thanks for the loaves, break them, and distribute them, along with the fish, to feed more than five thousand men, women, and children.

I love this picture of Jesus — taking the small loaves and raising them to heaven and thanking his Father. It was as though he were saying, "Whatever you give, Father, is enough to do the job." And it was. The disciples kept handing out the bread and the fish, and the people kept eating. At the end of the day, everyone was full and twelve baskets of food were left over — one for each disciple.

Jesus and his disciples had been tired, sick at heart, longing for some peace and quiet. The last thing they desired was to spend the day with an endless stream of people, each one expecting a miracle. But once again the love and compassion of Jesus prevailed. What an experience his disciples must have had as their concern gave way to confusion, and confusion to wonder, and wonder to joy. Five small loaves had fed a multitude and they themselves had been instruments of the miracle, laughing as they dipped their hands into the baskets, scooping out fish and bread for the hungry.

Watching Jesus that day must have been quite an education in miracles. It would have taught the disciples about the power of combining gratitude with faith, and faith with brokenness — a mixture potent enough to make a miracle. Looking back years later, they must have thought about that day on the shore in light of the last meal they ate with Jesus before his death, when his body would be broken on a Roman cross. Then too he took the bread in his hands, gave thanks, and broke it, saying, "Take and eat. This is my body" (Matthew 26:26).

The brokenness of Jesus is all that any of us have to offer each other. But it is that very brokenness that is the yeast for miracles. When Jesus lives in me, and I in him, I have something to offer, no matter how small my gifts. It may seem that I have so little of what others need: money, patience, time, and love. But if I take what little I do have, give thanks for it, break it open, and give it away, then I too will help feed the hungry of this world.

Jesus, when I was desperate and sick in soul, you came to me. When I was confused and alone, you took pity on me. When I was your enemy, you laid down your life for me. Your brokenness has healed me and fed me and brought peace to my soul. And now you live within me by the power of your Spirit. When I am overwhelmed by the needs of others, wondering what I can do to help, let me remember the miracle of the loaves and fishes. Grant that I might be a small loaf that you take in your hands, break open, and hand out to those who are hungry.

A MIRACLE OF SOUP
AND BREAD

~≥~

By this time it was late in the day, so [Jesus'] disciples came to him. "This is a remote place," they said, "and it's already very late. Send the people away so they can go to the surrounding countryside and villages and buy themselves something to eat." But he answered, "You give them something to eat."

Mark 6:35 – 37

Paul Thigpen attended Yale University in the early seventies, an era disdainful of the supernatural. For many faith was an anachronism and miracles were merely the by-product of an overactive imagination. Given time, you could find a natural explanation for anything and everything that happened. Paul himself had been an atheist for six of his teenage years, and he too had thought that matter and energy were all that existed in the universe. But that all changed with his conversion at the end of his senior year of high school and a subsequent two-year stint on the mission field in Europe.

At Yale, Paul was a religious studies major. One of his religion courses, taught by a skeptical professor, seemed designed to destroy rather than nourish faith. At one point, his professor made a remark about the gospel account of the multiplication of the loaves and fishes that Paul would never forget. The instructor casually noted that the account was obviously not historical because everyone knew, of course, that miracles don't happen and that food can't actually be multiplied.

"I just shook my head," remembered Paul, "and thought about the remarkable things I had experienced on the mission field during the previous two years. Before my time in Europe, that kind of remark would have corroded my faith. But now it merely sounded presumptuous and foolish.

"As a missionary, I had lived in a little town called Nieder-Woellstadt, just north of Frankfurt, Germany, on staff at a training center for Christian youths.

"Before long, word got out to backpacking tourists that we would sometimes provide free meals to those who dropped by. We often had last-minute dinner guests, but we didn't have much money for groceries. So we did what we could and hoped for the best. On a couple of occasions, the cook whispered to me: 'Paul, we just don't have enough soup and bread. Pray that God will either multiply the food or shrink our appetites.' So we prayed, and the food never ran out. The more times this happened, the more we wondered whether God was performing a miracle in our own small kitchen.

"Curiosity got the better of the two of us, so we decided to experiment. One day, we carefully measured the amount of soup in the pot and then measured how much of it we served. All the while, we watched to make sure that nobody poured water into the soup to thin it out and make it last longer. After dinner, we realized that our suspicions were true. We had, indeed, ladled out more soup than we had made.

"In addition to soup, we often served the kind of thick-crusted dark bread that is so popular in Germany. I decided to repeat the experiment. One night when our bread supply didn't match our needs for supper, I carefully measured the length of a loaf before I put it through the slicing machine. Then I reassembled it so that the slices were packed hard against each other and remeasured the bread. Just as before, the impossible had happened! The loaf was several inches longer than it had been before I sliced it.

"It's been more than twenty years since I witnessed these miracles. But they are still so vivid. I realize I can't prove anything to the world, but neither can I ignore the evidence of my own eyes."

I wonder if it takes more faith to believe that God *can* multiply food or more faith to believe that he would bother doing so. After all, why should he go to the trouble to perform a miracle simply to fill the bellies of a few hungry backpackers? Perhaps he was making a point—that the Jesus who worked miracles two thousands years ago is the same Jesus who works miracles today. Across the centuries two things have remained the same: the nature of our needs and the all-surpassing power of our God to meet them. Paul Thigpen knows that God can do whatever he wants, whenever he wants, through whomever he chooses.

Father, forgive me for the times I have tried to hem you in with my skepticism, to fashion a god after my own understanding. Open me to miracles, Lord, and give me a robust faith. Reveal your greatness, and then let me simply bow down and adore you.

THE MIRACLE OF TOO MANY FISH

❧

[Jesus] said to Simon, "Put out into deep water, and let down the nets for a catch." Simon answered, "Master, we've worked hard all night and haven't caught anything. But because you say so, I will let down the nets." When they had done so, they caught such a large number of fish that their nets began to break.

Luke 5:4–6

Everyone knew that the best time to fish was at night. Simon Peter had been at it for hours with nothing to show for his labors. As the morning sun crept over the hills and skimmed across the Sea of Galilee, he decided he might as well dock the boat and hope for better luck tomorrow. As he was cleaning his nets, the man called Jesus decided to use his boat for a pulpit, asking Peter to put out a little from shore so he would have a better vantage point from which to address the crowd. Peter liked this Jesus. The rabbi had been to his home and prayed for his mother-in-law, who had been suffering from a high fever. He was unlike any teacher he had ever heard, telling story after story that seemed to turn the world and everything in it upside down.

Suddenly Peter realized that Jesus was talking to him. "Put out into deep water, and let down the nets for a catch." Peter respected the man as a teacher, but what did he know about fishing? He and his crew had worked hard through the night and had caught nothing. Still, he did as Jesus asked. Though he knew it to be an exercise in futility, Peter gave the signal to drop the nets and then slowly to raise them. His muscles straining as he heaved and pulled on the ropes, it seemed to Peter as though he were attempting to raise the floor of the sea itself. At last, the nets surfaced, bulging and tearing, unable to contain so many fish. Peter called frantically to his partners to bring their boat alongside to help harvest the catch. The boats were heaped so high with fish that they began to sink.

Peter was overwhelmed by the miracle, not because of his good fortune, but because of what he was beginning to realize about the One who worked the miracle. He fell at Jesus' knees, begging him to leave him. "God away from me, Lord; I am a sinful man!" But Jesus merely said, "Don't be afraid; from now on you will catch men" (Luke 5:8, 10).

Peter had worked hard through an entire evening with nothing at all to show for his efforts. It was precisely at that point that Jesus chose to perform a miracle, and Peter himself was caught in the net that Jesus cast forth. Later, he would lead many into the early church, thus fulfilling Jesus' words about him. The most Peter had been hoping for that day was a good catch of fish to supply the morning's market. But Jesus had bigger plans. By calling Peter and the other disciples, he was weaving a net to catch the souls of countless men and women through the ages.

Lord, I sometimes forget that I can do nothing of any significance without you. All my labors, my worrying, my staying up late, and getting up early will get me nowhere if you are not leading me. Help me to remember that you alone are the one who can make me fruitful. Whenever I am tempted to limit your work in and through me, remind me of the too-many fish in the too-few nets, and help me to cast my nets when and where you say to.

A MIRACLE AND MONEY

Give, and it will be given to you. A good measure, pressed down, shaken together and running over, will be poured into your lap. For with the measure you use, it will be measured to you.

Luke 6:38

Five dollars is a fortune if you don't have much money in your pocket. Debbi Moore had just enough for groceries that day. Family finances had been especially pinched lately, and she always shopped with cash. That way, she would be certain not to spend even a nickel more than she could afford.

On her way to the supermarket, she noticed a disheveled man standing by the side of the road. He wasn't begging for money, but only holding a sign that read, "Jesus Heals a Broken Heart." Debbi wasn't sure why, but she experienced an overwhelming urge to give him something, though she could little afford it.

She reached into the glove compartment of her car and drew out a five dollar bill. "It seemed like a lot to me," she explained, "but I knew I should give it to him. Still, I had a little problem ... I can look you dead in the eye, aim a Frisbee at you, and hit fifty yards to your left. I wasn't sure how I was going to get the money to the man on the sidewalk. The light was turning, and I knew the cars behind me might suck the bill under their wheels. So I said, 'This one's for you, Lord. You've got to get it there.' Then I crumpled it up and threw it out the passenger window. As I drove past, a glance in my side mirror showed the man's foot on the five dollar bill.

"After that I forgot all about it. But the next night I attended a prayer meeting and someone handed me an envelope. Inside was a gift certificate for twenty dollars to a local grocery store. In front of the certificate was a crisp five dollar bill!"

That day, Debbi Moore made an investment that Wall Street would kill for. She got a four hundred percent return on her money in less than forty-eight hours. Though Debbi didn't give because she was expecting anything in return, the gift in the envelope confirmed her belief that it is impossible to outdo the generosity of God.

Her story brings to mind the counsel of Jesus himself: "Give, and it will be given to you. A good measure, pressed down, shaken together and running over, will be poured into your lap. For with the measure you use, it will be measured to you." But Jesus wasn't just talking about money. Before making this statement, reported in the gospel of Luke, he says that if we don't want to be judged, we should refrain from judging, and if we want to be forgiven, then we should forgive others. The point is to be as generous as possible in our dealings with others—to show mercy, to go the extra mile, to give the benefit of the doubt, to extend a helping hand. It's not complicated; it's simply living out the Golden Rule in everyday terms.

Lord, living life on spiritual terms isn't nearly as complex as I sometimes make it. In essence, it simply means obeying your two great commands: to love you with all my heart, soul, and mind, and to love others as myself. Help me to keep these two things constantly in focus and let every other concern recede into the background.

THE MIRACLE OF OIL

Elisha said [to the widow], "Go around and ask all your
neighbors for empty jars. Don't ask for just a few. Then go
inside and shut the door behind you and your sons. Pour oil
into all the jars, and as each is filled, put it to one side."

2 Kings 4:3 – 5

Once upon a time in ancient Israel, there was a poor widow whose creditors were threatening to take her two sons as slaves if she didn't pay her husband's debts. Back then, you couldn't keep your creditors at bay simply by declaring bankruptcy. It was pay up or put up. And it looked like the latter, until the prophet Elisha came to her rescue.

It seems that the widow's husband had been in the same line of work as Elisha. So it was to Elisha she went with her troubles. As soon as he heard of her dilemma, he asked how he could help. "What do you have in your house?" he probed.

"Your servant has nothing at all," she said, "except a little oil." That's when he told her to start knocking on doors to collect all the jars she could get her hands on. So she and her sons did just that. Then he told her to start pouring the oil into the jars. She poured and she poured and she poured some more until every jar was filled to the brim. It wasn't until the very last jar had been topped off that she ran out of oil.

Now in those days the kind of oil you had in your kitchen was worth a lot of money. Since she had so much of it, the widow sold the excess, made more than enough money to pay off her debts, and she and her sons lived happily ever after. Thanks to a miracle, what little she had was more than enough to save the day.

Unlike the widow, I have never had the misfortune of being in debt up to my ears. The wolf has never stood howling at my door. And the bank has never threatened to repossess anything, not even my car. I have been greatly blessed, and I know it.

But it is one thing to have money in the bank and another to have enough spiritual capital in your soul. The truth is that I often lack both the emotional and spiritual resources that seem so necessary to daily life — patience, time, perspective, energy, confidence, wisdom, understanding, forgiveness, faith, hope for the future. Perhaps you can identify with my list. Or maybe you have a list of your own.

The point of the widow's story is that God can take what little we have and multiply it if we ask and have faith. Elisha encouraged the widow to exercise her faith by requiring her to borrow as many jars as she could in which to store the oil. But when she went knocking on doors, she still had only a little oil in her possession. It was the same with Noah when God instructed him to make an ark. He had to build the boat before even a drop of water had fallen from the sky.

This doesn't mean that God will answer every one of our prayers precisely as we want him to if we will only have enough faith. He may assess our needs differently than we do, allowing some of them to go unmet or to wait awhile so that he can work out a deeper purpose in our lives.

Whatever the case, life goes much better with faith. If you feel that you have too little of this precious commodity, ask God to multiply it. And if you haven't already done so, pray for his Spirit to indwell you. Interestingly enough, oil is actually a symbol for the Holy Spirit. And it is the Spirit who gives us life, enabling us to have faith in a God who will meet our deepest needs, no matter how impossibly desperate we feel.

Father, thank you for the new day. For the sun that scatters red and green and gold across the earth to make our world beautiful. For the trees that keep the soil from blowing away and the hills that make life interesting. For the fuel in our stoves, the food on our table, and the hope in our hearts. For one another. For your Spirit. We thank you. Help us to be glad for all that you have given. And so increase our faith for all that you intend to give us still.

15

MIRACLES OF LIFE AND DEATH

❧

There are only two ways to live your life. One is as though nothing is a miracle. The other is as if everything is.

Albert Einstein

When I was a child, someone gave me an unusual necklace. It was a round globe of glass attached to a silver chain. Inside the glass was a small seed. I loved peering at the seed, wondering how it got trapped inside the glass. But to tell the truth, I would have liked it even better had the glass encased something really interesting—like a bumble bee or a mosquito. I didn't realize that my new bauble was supposed to remind me of the words of Jesus: "I tell you the truth, if you have faith as small as a mustard seed, you can say to this mountain, 'Move from here to there' and it will move. Nothing will be impossible for you" (Matthew 17:20).

But what are these mountains Jesus speaks of? Is he encouraging us to start rearranging the surrounding landscape, moving mountains as we would the furniture in our living rooms? Somehow I doubt it. Instead, I think he is saying that even the tiniest amount of faith can create spiritual earthquakes. These earthquakes sometimes happen in families, where one person prays for the conversion of the rest. Or in communities, where different individuals are touched by God's power and his love. Sometime they involve matters of life and death, and at other times they shake things up more gradually and quietly.

If you know of particular mountains that need moving, remember the role that faith plays. As you read the stories that follow, I hope they will strengthen the faith you already have so that you, too, will experience a miracle in your own life.

A DEATH-DEFYING MIRACLE

⤙⤚

"Take away the stone," he said. "But, Lord," said Martha, the sister of the dead man, "by this time, there is a bad odor, for he has been there four days." Then Jesus said, "Did I not tell you that if you believed, you would see the glory of God?" So they took away the stone.... Jesus called in a loud voice, "Lazarus, come out!" The dead man came out, his hands and feet wrapped with strips of linen, and a cloth around his face. Jesus said to them, "Take off the grave clothes and let him go."
John 11:39–41, 43–44

I came face to face with death for the first time when I was nine years old. And I didn't like what I saw. My father's mother had died and we arrived at the funeral home to pay our respects. Shortly after we got there, I saw my grandfather lean over the casket and kiss my grandmother, lying so still and pale. I suppose it was a tender moment, but it frightened me. Someone asked whether I would like to kiss her, but I said no. The thick makeup spread over her skin only made her look gray and cold as a stone. The best I could do was recite a quiet prayer in front of her casket.

The next day, we arrived at my grandfather's house before the funeral. As soon as I walked through the door, I was struck speechless. There on the couch sat my grandmother, fifty pounds lighter, but full of life! I could hear her voice again, recognize the familiar gesture as she flicked the too-long ashes from her cigarette. Her skin looked pink and fresh and soft against her raven hair. But before I could rush over and throw my arms around her, someone introduced her as my Great Aunt Leonore. I hadn't even known my grandmother had a sister, let alone one that looked just like her. Of course I was glad to meet my aunt but crushed by my childish mistake. People don't rise from the dead, after all. What had I been thinking?

But I have since come to believe that sometimes people do rise from the grave. Unlike me, Martha and Mary didn't suffer a case of mistaken identity. Their brother Lazarus really had walked out of his tomb, slow and stiff, to be sure. But there was no question he was alive again.

Still, they had doubted Jesus for the miracle. Mary had thrown herself at Jesus' feet, weeping because he had arrived too late to heal her brother. And Martha had balked when he ordered the stone removed from the tomb. "Lord, don't you realize he's been dead for four days? He'll stink if you open the tomb!" But Jesus insisted—and the impossible happened.

This incredible miracle is a sign of hope for every follower of Christ in every age of the church. Without the assurance that we will live forever, healing would have little value. It would only be a delaying tactic, staving off annihilation for a few moments, days, or years. Inevitably, our hearts will one day stop, our lungs will pump their last molecule of oxygen, and our brains will be incapable of one more thought. But that won't be the end of us. Because the Spirit of Jesus dwells in us, we will hear his voice beckoning, and our last enemy, death, will finally be swallowed up by life. When that happens, I plan on sitting down beside my grandmother, throwing my arms around her, and telling her just how glad I am to see her.

Jesus, it's no wonder Mary and Martha had a hard time believing. But all you asked was that they have enough faith to roll away the stone from the tomb. Please forgive my skepticism and remove the stone of unbelief from my heart. When the time comes, grant me the grace of a peaceful death.

THE MIRACLE OF
A HAPPY DEATH

❧

Are not two sparrows sold for a penny? Yet not one of them
will fall to the ground apart from the will of your Father. And
even the very hairs of your head are all numbered. So don't be
afraid; you are worth more than many sparrows.

Matthew 10:29–31

Joan Lindeman and her husband, Don, lived in Almond, New York. They had been married forty years, but their time together was drawing to a close. Six months earlier, Don had tentatively been diagnosed with Alzheimer's disease. The prognosis was horrifying. In Joan's mind, the future loomed like a living death sentence for him. Alive in body but so far away in spirit.

Joan's sense of loss was sharpened by the fact that one of her sons had been killed just two weeks before she moved Don into a nursing home twenty miles away. Every afternoon she made the trip to see him. Tears salted her prayers as she crossed and recrossed the twenty miles that separated them. Knowing that Alzheimer's patients often live for many years, she cried out to God, asking him to spare Don from this long misery. "The day he doesn't know me will be the saddest day of my life," she thought.

"One morning I was speaking to my son who lives in Florida. He knew the stress I had been under and would call frequently to see how his dad and I were faring. It was such a comfort to talk with him that we would usually chat for a half hour or more. But shortly after he called, I had an irresistible urge to hang up and leave for the nursing home. As soon as I put the phone down, my daughter-in-law called. She was still grieving the loss of her husband, my other son. I was so aware of her pain that I hated to cut her short, but I just knew I had to get to the nursing home. 'This doesn't make any sense,' I thought to myself. 'Don was fine when I left him yesterday. But I'm sure he needs me.'

"As soon as I arrived, a nurse hailed me. Donald was ill. The doctor who had just examined him couldn't explain why his temperature had suddenly spiked. Perhaps he was struggling with a bout of the flu.

"I rushed into his room, shocked to see my husband lying in bed, his face the color of bleached linen and glistening with sweat. Without a word, he grasped my hand and looked into my eyes for reassurance. I spoke lovingly to him, patting the moisture from his face. Then he died in my arms.

"Had I ignored the feeling that he needed me, I would have missed the chance to be with Don when he died. It was heartbreaking to lose him, but I was comforted by the thought that his sufferings had been brief and that we had been together the moment he left this earth. The doctors had thought he would live for many years, but God, in his mercy, had other plans. By some miracle of divine radar, God let me tune in to what was happening so that I could be there when Don needed me most."

Father, death is never easy. Often it is an ugly and painful experience. Frightening for those who die and for those who are left behind. But it comforts me to know that you do not abandon us when it's time to pass from this world to the next.

You mark the moment with your mercy, assuring us that we are of more value to you than we can possibly imagine. Give us, we ask, a death that is full of both your peace and your presence.

A CHILD'S MIRACLE

❦

*"For I know the plans I have for you," declares the LORD,
"plans to prosper you and not to harm you, plans to give you
hope and a future."*

Jeremiah 29:11

It was 1955. Dr. Jonas Salk was the man of the year in America. His miracle vaccine was about to put an end to the terror that stalked the world's children, crippling or killing hundreds of thousands of children during each successive epidemic. Thanks to Salk, polio would soon become as rare in the developed world as the bubonic plague. Millions of children across the United States would be the first to benefit.

Unfortunately, Marilyn Graven Smith wasn't one of them. The child of American missionaries, she was excitedly awaiting Christmas at home in Phnom Penh, Cambodia. Neither she nor her parents had the slightest hint of the anguish they would endure in the next few days.

"I was sitting in the living room one Monday night when my neck suddenly began to stiffen up. It was so tight I couldn't even move it. My head ached, I was feverish, and when I tried to talk, the words tumbled out in a slur. On Tuesday, my father took me to our family doctor, who immediately admitted me to the hospital. He suspected polio, but tried to soften the blow by saying that it might be meningitis.

"On Wednesday morning a French specialist, who was touring Asia to study the outbreak of polio, stopped by to see me and later confirmed the diagnosis. It was bulbar polio.

"Simultaneously, the field chairman for the mission wired the national office in New York, asking people to pray for ten-year-old Marilyn Graven, who wasn't expected to live. Telegrams flew across continents and people throughout the world begged God for a miracle.

"By Wednesday night my right side was paralyzed from the neck down and no one could understand a word of what I said. I didn't know it, but when I went to sleep that night, none of the hospital staff expected me to wake up the next day.

"When my doctor walked into my room Thursday morning, he was astonished to see me sitting up in bed, talking a blue streak in much-improved English. As a further test, he asked me to get out of bed and walk to the door. I was so eager to prove I was well that I ran across the room and nearly toppled over in the process. Of course I was still weak from the last few days, but the paralysis had definitely disappeared.

"My family doctor was an agnostic, but when Dad asked him whether my recovery was a miracle, he simply shook his head and replied, 'Without doubt, without doubt.' Word of my case soon spread throughout Southeast Asia. I had survived a terrible killer through the power of prayer.

"I knew with certainty that God had saved my life that night. The child of missionaries, I was often asked by well-meaning adults whether I planned to become one when I grew up. My answer was always swift and definite. The last thing I would ever be was a missionary. I didn't even want to consider it. But when God healed me, I realized the future wasn't entirely mine to decide. He had kept me alive for a reason. Somehow I knew he had a plan for my life, and I didn't want to miss it. Before long, I started to warm to the idea of missionary work. Eventually, I ended up serving with my husband in Peru and Ecuador."

Marilyn Graven was a blessed little girl. Through the mercy of a loving God and the power of prayer, polio was robbed of one of its victims. Her story reminds us that no matter how desperate our present circumstances, God himself cups the future in his hands.

Father, you hold the world and all its children within your grasp. You created each of us from nothing, and you love the work of your hands. When we are tempted to despair, let us remember that you are the Lord of both life and death. Not even a sparrow falls to the ground without your knowing it. With that assurance, let us surrender to the future, believing that whether we live or whether we die, you will keep us safe.

A MIRACLE OF HOPE

~≈~

May the God of hope fill you with all joy and peace as you trust in him, so that you may overflow with hope by the power of the Holy Spirit.

Romans 15:13

Brad and Judy Fletcher had decided to move to a larger city from a rural community twenty-five miles away. "We made an offer on a house three doors down from our friends Bob and Liz," Brad explained, "but the deal fell through because our house was slow to sell. Meanwhile, someone else bought the home we had hoped to move into. But Liz and Judy wouldn't give up. On the Fourth of July, they passed out fliers in the neighborhood advertising our interest. When they passed 3612 Frederick St., Judy stopped for a moment and said, 'That's the house were supposed to have. I don't know how I know, but I do.'

"One Saturday in September we received a surprise call from the owners of that home. Sure enough the second sale had fallen through. Had our house sold yet? It had and we were interested. The closing date was set for October 29. Had I known then what I know now, I would have chosen a different date.

"For several months I had been working on a multimillion-dollar deal on behalf of my company. Soon I discovered that the closing date for the wire transfer of funds was also set for October 29 — in Baltimore. The timing was less than ideal, but my father agreed to take my place and accompany Judy to the closing for our new home.

"The evening of October 28, Judy took our daughters, Julie and Kelly, out to dinner to celebrate. As soon as they returned home, Judy became ill with what she thought was either the flu or food poisoning. But it was something far worse. By morning she was lying on the floor vomiting. She was in so much pain that she begged God to let her die. Fortunately, a business associate stopped by the house to drop off some papers related to the closing. He became alarmed when he saw Judy and called me in Baltimore. I spoke to Judy on the phone and could tell that something was terribly wrong with her. She was disoriented and didn't seem to know what was going on. We arranged for her to get to the hospital immediately, and I left to catch the first plane home.

"I braced myself as I entered the hospital. For a moment, I felt as though I had accidentally stepped onto a movie set in the middle of its most tragic scene. The family was in tears. A social worker was there to help prepare the girls for the worst. And the hospital staff was trying to keep the patient alive until her husband arrived to spend precious last minutes alone with his wife.

"Judy's doctor explained that she was in a coma and on life support. She went into respiratory arrest while she was being examined in the emergency room. Had she arrived a few minutes later, we would have already been discussing the funeral. The diagnosis was spinal meningitis. She had hydrocephalus, which was putting enormous pressure on her brain. He hoped to relieve the pressure by inserting shunts.

"I had served in a medical intensive care unit during my stint in the navy. When I entered Judy's room for the first time, I couldn't help but think that some of the people we had lost in that unit looked better than she did.

"Afterward, I took Julie and Kelly to the chapel to pray. 'Kids, your mother is going to live, although we don't know where yet. She will either live with us in our new home, or she will live with Jesus in heaven. Let's pray for healing, strength, and the grace to accept God's will.'

"By Saturday the doctor informed me that most patients in Judy's condition either died or suffered severe brain damage, causing minimal quality of life. He warned me that I might need to face the decision of whether to take her off life support.

"But neither I nor anyone else was willing to give up hope. Friends rented a van and moved our things into our home. Casseroles appeared on our doorstep. People showed up to rake leaves and clean house. Men and women all over the city were praying for Judy's recovery. Entire congregations were interceding and before long the Judy Fletcher prayer chain stretched across several states. Fortunately, our new home was just five minutes from the hospital, and our neighbor, Liz, became like a second mother to our daughters. God had indeed earmarked that house on Frederick Street as our new home. Our little family had never realized there was so much love in the world.

"But Judy's coma persisted. By late November, her neurosurgeon explained that he had two alternatives: he could try a drug that might stop the swelling in her brain but would probably cause her to become a permanent invalid or he could remove part of her brain to make room for more swelling, thus buying time against the disease. As someone who always carefully considers his options, I pressed hard for a third alternative. Her doctor gave it to me: 'He could do nothing, and she would die.' I chose option two.

"On Thanksgiving Day he operated, and family and friends gathered in the waiting room still praying for a miracle. In an act of faith, one of our friends showed up with a Christmas tree, a string, and some popcorn. She put us to work making the decorations. It was her way of saying that Judy would survive the operation and that we might as well decorate the tree in preparation for Christmas. While the surgeon was in one room trying to save Judy's life, this woman was in another trying to save us from despair.

"Judy survived the operation. After forty-five days, she emerged from her coma. The Christmas season arrived, and I had the joy of seeing her lifted from bed and placed in a wheelchair for the first time since she entered the hospital. It was both a beautiful and pathetic sight. Judy looked as though she had just come in second in a bullfight. But I received the best Christmas gift anyone could ever ask for. I had the joy of wheeling my wife out of intensive care in order to show off the Christmas tree we had decorated for her on Thanksgiving.

"Before long, she was in a rehabilitation unit, though her prognosis was still dismal. But we refused to stop hoping for a total cure. By March the light at the end of the tunnel became visible. She could take a few steps without assistance, her hair had grown into a fashionable butch cut, and she could carry on a coherent conversation. To everyone's amazement, she recovered fully except for some short-term memory loss. When I asked the nurses and doctors who they thought was responsible for her cure, not one of them claimed credit. They simply pointed toward heaven when asked about her remarkable recovery.

"Finally, 155 days after the onset of her illness, I took Judy home. It was Good Friday, April 1, 1988. But we immediately renamed it 'Great Friday.'"

Lord, in the midst of tragedy, we pray for the grace to hold on to two things: our hope in you and our love for one another. With these two gifts, we will taste victory, no matter what happens.

A MIRACLE OF LIFE

~

You created my inmost being;
*   you knit me together in my mother's womb.*
I praise you because I am fearfully and wonderfully made.

Psalm 139:13 – 14

I wasn't supposed to be born," explains John Drahos. "My mother was partially paralyzed and nearly totally bedridden with multiple sclerosis when her doctor told her she was pregnant. She was delighted with the news. After three failed pregnancies, she was longing for a child.

"But her doctor was so worried that his bedside manner failed him completely. 'If you decide to carry this baby to term, you're going to have to find another doctor,' he told her. 'I'm not going to stand by and watch you give birth to a baby you can't possibly care for. Furthermore, you know as well as I do that this child might be physically or mentally handicapped. You can't take the kind of medicine you've been on without suffering the consequences.'

"But my mother was determined: 'This child is a human being whose life I have no right to take. If it *is* malformed, then my husband and I will give it that much more love, and we will find a way to care for the baby.'

"She wouldn't budge, and so I was born. I had all ten fingers and toes, two eyes, a nose, and, according to my mother, the most beautiful smile in the world. I did suffer from some minor health problems, but soon I was as well as any normal child.

"Best of all, immediately after I was born, my mother experienced a total remission from her MS, which lasted for seven years! She was so energetic that she even chased me up and down the terraced lawns behind our house when I was young and full of mischief.

"In today's overheated debate about abortion, one rarely thinks of the issue from the child's viewpoint. That's why I'm so glad to tell my story. Were it not for my mother's reverence for human life and her courage in challenging the 'medical wisdom' of her doctor, I would never have known the intoxicating smell of a freshly cut rose, the glow of moonlight on a green lawn, or the loving touch of another human being. I would have missed the miracle that is life."

Father, because you knit us together in our mothers' wombs, our lives have meaning and eternal significance. Help us to live every day conscious of the sacredness of life. As this reverence deepens, may we treat each other accordingly, with dignity and respect, with love and mercy, just as you treat us.

16

MIRACLES OF DELIVERANCE

❦

This poor man called, and the LORD heard him;
he saved him out of all his troubles.
The angel of the LORD encamps around those who fear him,
and he delivers them.

Psalm 34:6–7

It's a wonder I love animals. When I was four years old, I was pinned to the ground by a vicious Great Dane. If my life flashed in front of me then, it was too short to remember the experience. But I will never forget the vision of menacing teeth and angry eyes poised an inch above my nose. Nor will I forget the relief I felt when my older brother rescued me and chased the monster away.

That's how I feel when I think about the way God delivers his people. Scripture warns us to be on guard because our enemy, the devil, prowls around like a roaring lion seeking someone to devour. I don't know about you, but the thought that I could be eaten alive is enough to ruin my day. In fact, I've always been grateful that humans are at the top of the food chain rather than somewhere further down.

But in the spiritual world the unhappy truth is that we are beset by predators. Fortunately, we are protected from such enemies by a power far greater than theirs. As long as we believe in Christ, we need not fear. All that our Deliverer asks is that we cooperate with him through our faith and by living in obedience to him. Knowing this, we can exult with the psalmist:

Even though I walk
through the valley of the shadow of death,
I will fear no evil,
for you are with me;
your rod and your staff,
they comfort me.
You prepare a table before me
in the presence of my enemies.
You anoint my head with oil;
my cup overflows.

Surely goodness and love will follow me
  all the days of my life,
and I will dwell in the house of the LORD
  forever.

Psalm 23:4–6

THE MIRACLE OF TOO MANY FROGS

If you refuse to let [the Israelites] go, I will plague your whole country with frogs. The Nile will teem with frogs. They will come up into your palace and your bedroom and onto your bed, into the houses of your officials and on your people, and into your ovens and kneading troughs.

Exodus 8:2–3

For more years than they could remember, the Israelites had been slaves in Egypt. They spoke to one another about the fathers of their race—of Abraham, Isaac, and Jacob, and of Joseph who had once been great in Egypt and who, on his deathbed, had prophesied their deliverance. It was said that these men conversed with God himself.

But God was silent now. Silent, that is, until Moses, the Hebrew son of Pharaoh's daughter, returned from his exile in the desert, claiming to have talked with God. He spoke of freedom from the tyranny of Egypt and of a promised land where they would dwell in peace and security. And now he and his brother, Aaron, were matching wits with Pharaoh's magicians, attempting to convince the tyrant to let God's people go.

But Pharaoh was stubborn. He refused to listen to Moses and Aaron, even after they changed the Nile River to blood. Now they promised a plague of frogs if Pharaoh would not relent. And he would not. So the frogs came in thousands and covered the land. They were everywhere—in ovens, on beds, underfoot, and even in the bread and water. Then, just as suddenly as they had appeared, the frogs died. From one end of the nation to the other, Egypt reeked of them.

The Israelites must have enjoyed the irony of this plague. They knew that the Egyptians worshiped the frog as a sacred idol, the god of fecundity. Now the God of Israel was rubbing their noses in their idolatry. Where was this mighty god of Egypt when the true God displayed his power?

Scripture tells us that after the frogs died, Pharaoh hardened his heart, refusing to listen to Moses and Aaron. Throughout the Bible, "hardening the heart" involves rejecting God in favor of something else. While obedience softens the heart, sin hardens it. The more the heart disregards its Creator, the less susceptible it will be to grace. With each plague, Pharaoh's heart grew harder and more distant from God.

Clearly, Pharaoh was one of history's bad guys. If we identify with anyone in the story, it's likely to be Moses or the oppressed Israelites. Yet, in common with Pharaoh, we share a heart that is capable of either great good or enormous evil. And like him, we sometimes suffer judgment. We may not wake up with frogs on our pillow, but we will inevitably sample the consequences of our sin. If we drink too much, we will one day find that alcohol has robbed us of our family and our future. If we are disloyal, we may one day face betrayal. If we have judged harshly, we will search in vain for mercy when we need it most. True, we don't always get exactly what we deserve. But sooner or later we usually do get a taste of our own medicine. Bitter though it is, this is the medicine that has the power to deliver us from evil, to heal our hearts and keep them soft.

Father, you tell us that you discipline everyone whom you accept as a son or daughter. When you correct me, help me to realize you are simply treating me as a member of the family. Let me respond in a way that makes my heart as different from Pharaoh's as summer is from winter and as day is from night. Give me grace to admit my sin and ask your forgiveness. As I do, soften my heart and fill it with your presence.

DELIVER ME FROM EVIL

Submit yourselves, then, to God. Resist the devil, and he will flee from you. Come near to God and he will come near to you.

James 4:7–8

Some things never change. It doesn't matter whether you're talking about ancient Palestine, modern-day America, or somewhere in Asia seventy years ago. The war between good and evil still rages—sometimes in dramatic ways.

George Soltau explains that his father lived in South Korea in the early 1920s. T. Stanley Soltau was an itinerant Presbyterian missionary, traveling from one village church to another. He would carry his own food and bedding and spend a short time in each place, performing various ministerial duties: examining candidates for baptism, conducting communion services, and preaching.

"Most of his duties were rather routine," explained George. "But there were always surprises. One day he entered a small village only to be greeted by a group of excited men and women. 'Pastor, please come quickly,' they implored. 'We have a woman who is demon-possessed.' When he arrived at the church he saw her. She was raving obscenities, cursing, and writhing uncontrollably. Inexperienced in such matters, he recalled how such incidents were described in the Gospels. He quickly organized a prayer team of people who promised to pray around the clock for her. By early evening the exorcism was complete. The demon left and the woman went absolutely limp.

"The next day he made his way over the mountain into the next little valley. As soon as he arrived, the people rushed toward him, telling him that one of the women had become demon-possessed. Just like the other woman, she was ranting and cursing. The villagers had tied her hands so that she couldn't hurt herself or anyone else. Again a prayer team was organized and the woman was set free. When the pastor inquired about the time that she began acting as though she were possessed, he discovered that it was about the same time that the previous woman had been delivered!"

T. Stanley Soltau didn't need to look far for an explanation. He certainly would have recalled the many encounters Jesus had with demonized individuals. He may have even recalled the words of the apostle Peter: "Be self-controlled and alert. Your enemy the devil prowls around like a roaring lion looking for someone to devour. Resist him, standing firm in the faith" (1 Peter 5:8–9). He didn't know the two women well enough to know why they had been such easy targets for demonic powers. But he did know that the power of Jesus to deliver them was far stronger than the power of evil to enslave them.

Few of us encounter evil undisguised. Most often it masks itself in subtler disguises. Whatever the case, we needn't fear it as long as we stand firm in faith, calling on the Father to lead us not into temptation and to deliver us from every form of evil.

Lord, I reject Satan and all his works and empty promises. I believe you are God, the Father almighty, Creator of heaven and earth. I believe in Jesus Christ, your only Son and my Lord, who died and who rose from the dead. I believe in the

Holy Spirit, the resurrection of the body, and life everlasting. Thank you for giving me the grace to believe. Watch over and protect me from every form of evil. And grant that I might live in your presence forever. Amen.

THE MIRACLE OF THE BOY AND THE GIANT

As the Philistine moved closer to attack him, David ran quickly toward the battle line to meet him. Reaching into his bag and taking out a stone, he slung it and struck the Philistine on the forehead. The stone sank into his forehead, and he fell facedown on the ground. So David triumphed over the Philistine with a sling and a stone; without a sword in his hand he struck down the Philistine and killed him.

1 Samuel 17:48–50

Pitting David against Goliath would have been like sending a glider into battle with a Stealth Bomber. The boy with the slingshot didn't have a chance against a nine-foot colossus, wearing 125 pounds of bronze armor. But we all know that David got his man despite the odds.

This story, familiar to many of us since our childhood, conjures up proverbs like, "Pride cometh before destruction," and "The bigger they are, the harder they fall." And though we may not have thought about it for years, the miracle of David and Goliath is a story that reveals much about our struggle with evil.

You will remember that Goliath had challenged King Saul and the Jews to produce a champion to fight him. If the Jewish champion prevailed, the Philistines would become their subjects. But if Goliath won, the Israelites would become their slaves. For forty days, the giant taunts them, and each day their fear increases as he grows larger and more hideous in their eyes. His threats weave a spell over the Israelites. He is like a spider toying with its prey.

Then David breaks upon the scene and exclaims with youthful indignation, "Who is this uncircumcised Philistine that he should defy the armies of the living God?" Was this courage on the boy's part or stupidity? Knowing the end of the story helps us to tell the difference.

A thousand years later, the story repeats itself, not far from where David fought Goliath. This time the battle takes place in the desert outside Jerusalem and the threatening giant is none other than the devil himself. In the Hebrew Scriptures, the devil is represented by figures like Goliath and Pharaoh, but in the Gospels he comes on the scene undisguised.

Like David, who stripped himself of Saul's protecting armor and sword, Jesus strips himself of bodily strength by fasting. David faced Goliath after forty days of the giant's threats. Now Jesus meets Satan after forty days in the desert. David battled Goliath with only a stone and a sling, while Jesus defeats Satan with only the Word of God.

Over and over the themes echo through Scripture and repeat themselves in the life of faith. God sends deliverance to his people, who are enslaved by sin and Satan. Weakness overcomes strength; humility defeats pride; faith confounds fear; light overcomes darkness. When hope appears to have vanished, victory breaks through. These are the paradoxes on which faith rests and the life of grace unfolds. As Christ says to Paul and as he says to us today: "My grace is sufficient for you, for my power is made perfect in weakness" (2 Corinthians 12:9).

Praise be to the Lord my Rock, who trains my hands for war, my fingers for battle. He is my loving God and my fortress, my stronghold and my deliverer, my shield, in whom I take refuge.

A MIRACLE IN THE NIGHT

He reached down from on high and took hold of me;
*   he drew me out of deep waters.*
He rescued me from my powerful enemy,
*   from my foes, who were too strong for me.*
They confronted me in the day of my disaster,
*   but the LORD was my support.*
He brought me out into a spacious place;
*   he rescued me because he delighted in me.*

Psalm 18:16–19

Carol Anderson didn't know what to do. Diagnosed with rheumatoid arthritis in 1978, her only escape from excruciating pain was a steady supply of codeine. She couldn't live without it, but her doctor told her she had to try. Otherwise, he couldn't perform the surgery she needed.

Her rheumatologist had been shocked by what he read on her X-rays. Her elbows had been completely eaten away by the disease. He had never seen so much destruction in a patient her age.

Carol knew she was hooked on an opiate and that she would have to endure the agony of withdrawal. She checked into a local drug-treatment center and was assigned to the detox unit. She tells her story in the November 1991 issue of *Charisma* magazine:

"I was insulted. They thought I was a junkie and put me on methadone. I looked at my crack-user roommate and piously informed God: 'I don't belong here. I took codeine for the pain.'"

She sensed his answer immediately: "You took drug for the pain in your arms. She took them for the pain in her heart. Don't think yourself better."

The detoxing process was far worse than she feared, complete with chills and night sweats, insomnia, and a sensation like insects crawling all over her body. Finally, one night she felt a presence in her room. "I knew it was the Lord," she explained. "I couldn't see Him with my physical eyes, but I could follow Him as He approached my bedside."

"I sang a song about God and me walking through the field together that I'd learned as a child.... I could feel Him clasp my hand. I could see us walking together."

That night was the beginning of the end of Carol's long nightmare. Her experience reassured her that God was still close by, holding tightly to her hand. After that, she began to hope that he would deliver her from pain and addiction. Shortly afterward, she was released from the treatment center, having kicked her codeine habit. But predictably, the pain returned. One day in church she went forward for prayer. She'd sought prayer so many times it almost seemed pointless. Still some stubbornness inside her refused to stop hoping for a miracle.

Afterward, her pain gradually receded and then disappeared completely. Before long, she found she could use her arms and hands to perform routine tasks like fastening buttons, combing her hair, or opening the clasp of a bracelet.

One day she strode into her surgeon's office, arms to her side, and asked whether he thought surgery was the only hope for restoring her. "He pointed impatiently at the X-rays. 'As I told you before, the damage is irreversible. Your elbows are destroyed. Your only hope is surgery.'

"I let him finish, then bent my arms up and down at the elbows. 'You mean if I don't have surgery, I won't be able to do this?'"

Carol's doctors couldn't explain what had happened to her. But she knew. The God who had taken hold of her hand in the middle of her darkest night was the one who had done the impossible and delivered her from the power of a terrible disease.

Lord, it's easy to believe in your love when the rays of the morning sun take the chill off our bodies and make us glad to be alive. But it's hard to keep faith in the middle of the night when every anxious thought is magnified and every pain is more acutely felt. Still, we know that faith often grows best in the dark. Even so, we ask you to reassure us of your presence when we are most tempted to believe you have abandoned us.

A MIRACLE OF
LIGHT AND DARK

Then the LORD said to Moses, "Stretch out your hand toward the sky so that darkness will spread over Egypt—darkness that can be felt." So Moses stretched out his hand toward the sky, and total darkness covered all Egypt for three days. No one could see anyone else or leave his place for three days. Yet all the Israelites had light in the places where they lived.

Exodus 10:21–23

Like many people, I am fascinated with caves, though I am not quite sure why. Perhaps some primordial nesting instinct is at work, stirring me to think of them as places of shelter and safety. Though caves can be a refuge, they can also be places of impenetrable darkness, particularly if you are unfortunate enough to be lost deep within one, without flashlight or fire to light the way.

This is how I imagine the Egyptians experiencing the palpable darkness that God sent to them as the ninth of ten plagues. They couldn't even see each other, let alone venture out of their homes for three full days. Worst of all, they had no way of knowing how long the darkness would endure.

Biblical scholars point out that Egypt had what was known as "the *khamsin* period." The *khamsin* was a type of westerly wind that would blow dense masses of fine sand from the desert, intercepting the sun's rays and creating a darkness so thick that it could be felt.

This kind of heavy darkness must have been particularly terrifying in the sun-drenched land of Egypt. It would be as though the sun suddenly slipped out of the California sky. To make matters worse, the darkness dealt a terrible blow to their religious beliefs. The Egyptians actually worshiped the sun god *Ra*. Now the God of the Israelite slaves was mocking their god with the darkness.

The remarkable thing about this plague is that the Israelites escaped the darkness completely. Goshen, the land where they lived, was bathed in sunlight. What a marvelous image of the deliverance God was accomplishing! Egypt itself was enthralled in the darkness of idol worship. Now God would consign them to their darkness. Israel, by contrast, belonged to the God who uttered these words at the creation of the world: "Let there be light." As Genesis 1:4 tells us, "God saw that the light was good, and he separated the light from the darkness."

Clearly, God was separating his people from the darkness of their bondage in Egypt. With each plague, his power became more apparent. In the end, Pharaoh succumbed to God's cry to "let my people go." And the long night of slavery was ended as the Israelites walked in freedom into the light of God's presence.

Deliver us, Lord, from every form of evil, especially the temptation to put anyone or anything above you. For this is nothing but the worship of idols, which leads only to darkness and death. May we not love children, spouse, security, wealth, freedom, comfort, power, beauty, or position more than we love you. For it is only by living in your presence that we continue to live in the light. You alone are the light of the world, the light that the darkness cannot overcome.

17

WHEN MIRACLES DON'T HAPPEN

❧

*Men's thirst for the most amazing and indubitable wonders
actually stems from a desire for a faith without shadows,
for a crown without a cross.... A miracle is Christian only if
it helps us to believe rather than relieves us of the necessity of faith.*

Louis Monden, S.J.

I'm a sucker for happy endings. I can enjoy a good novel that is full of tragic moments as long as things turn out reasonably well in the end. But woe to the author who strings me along and then lets me down with a bang. Most often, miracles are stories with tragic elements that have a happy ending. They appeal to our need for wonder and for mercy, for our longing to believe that God does hear our prayers and that he sometimes answers us in supernatural ways. If it were up to us, miracles would be as plentiful as butterflies in summer.

Louis Monden is the author of a fascinating book about miracles entitled *Signs and Wonders.* He offers yet another perspective on our thirst for miracles, pointing out that our desire often stems from an attempt to build a "faith without shadows." Just like the Jews in ancient Palestine, we clamor for "a sign from heaven." And like the apostle Thomas, we will believe only if we can touch and see the wounds of the risen Christ ourselves. But as Monden says, miracles merely help us "to believe rather than relieve us of the necessity of faith."

Despite our longings, we do not live in a perfect world. The promise of heaven is not yet fulfilled. As Monden points out, miracles "should not give the impression that this passing world is now already glorified, that Paradise has already been regained. The miracle must rather give a glimpse of what is to come; it is a kind of smile by which God lightens the path of his Church." What a wonderful image—a smile that lightens our path.

Scripture talks about life as a "valley of tears," and so it often is. But it is in the midst of tears and darkness that the deepest faith develops. Wherever and whenever miracles don't happen, we have an opportunity to allow faith to take root in our souls, and it is precisely this faith that has the power to work the deepest miracle of all, the one that happens quietly inside our own hearts.

If you have been asking for a miracle with no results, remember that God still loves you and hasn't forgotten you. Nor is he indifferent to your suffering. Don't let your faith depend on miracles, but instead, ask God to accomplish his purposes even if he doesn't answer your prayers in precisely the way you hope he will.

A FAITH
WITHOUT MIRACLES

*Now Thomas (called Didymus), one of the Twelve, was not with
the disciples when Jesus came. So the other disciples told him,
"We have seen the Lord!" But he said to them, "Unless I see the
nail marks in his hands and put my finger where the nails were,
and put my hand into his side, I will not believe it."*

John 20:24–25

Somehow, Thomas's skepticism comforts me. It reminds me that
I'm not the only doubter in the kingdom of God, the only one
who sometimes feels abandoned and confused.

It must have been easy enough for Thomas to believe when
he could sit across the table from Jesus, sharing the same loaf of
bread and drinking from the same cup, or when he could see the
sick healed and the dead raised. Even though the disciples of Jesus
had no money and no place to lay their heads at night, the work
was exhilarating. Word of Jesus' miracles had spread throughout
Israel. Each day, more followers were added to their number. Soon
they would be a force no power on earth could resist. And Thomas
would be there to see Israel restored, with a great king sitting on the
throne. It was wonderful to have a vision, for he knew that without
a vision the people would perish.

But Thomas's faith was shattered at Calvary. His hopes were
laid in the grave along with the body of Jesus. He must have felt

a terrible sense of grief, confusion, and loss—so much so that he seems to have responded angrily when the other disciples claimed to have seen the risen Jesus. "No, I refuse to believe you. Unless I see the nail marks with my own eyes and feel the wounds with my fingers, I will not believe."

It's easy to criticize Thomas for his unbelief. But if you have ever given heart and soul to some cause or some person only to be disappointed, you will understand his anger.

Sometimes our disappointment and disillusionment center on the church itself. We may have been part of a church that has fallen apart, destroyed by scandal or internal rivalries. We may have given the better part of our youth to some cause that has since been discredited or become distorted. Or perhaps we feel that God has abandoned us when we needed him most. A spouse has left; a child has died; a friend has turned her back on us. We have prayed for faith, for healing, for grace, but have been met with silence. We have asked for a cup of water and been given vinegar instead. When this happens, youthful idealism is in danger of evolving into cynicism. We don't want to believe again, to be tricked and fooled and disappointed. So we become angry in order to protect ourselves.

But our disappointment needn't make us allergic to faith. Thomas was disappointed because he did not understand Jesus and the real work he had come to do. Because he could not see why Jesus had to die, he could not at first believe in his resurrection.

Like Thomas's, our immature faith is not so much faith in Jesus as in a poster-like image of him that we have painted—someone who always acts lovingly as we define love; who answers our prayers, especially when they are reasonable; and who never does anything we can't understand. But the real Jesus refuses to let us settle for a false portrait of himself. One after the other, he keeps erasing our distorted pictures. It isn't as though Jesus has discarded love, faithfulness, and compassion from his palette. It's just that he adds deeper hues to them, so that eventually we will gaze on a Rembrandt rather than the stick-figure drawing we started with.

As our false images are shattered, we may see only darkness for a time. What used to comfort will comfort us no longer. We may even feel deeply disillusioned. But being disillusioned is a good thing if it means an illusory spell has been broken. If we cling to God during this time, our faith will return to us as a ripened fruit. We will enjoy deeper intimacy with Jesus and greater freedom and peace in our personal lives. The darkness will give way to light and we will know even as we are known.

Lord, just when I think I have you figured out, you upset everything. When will I learn that only the pure in heart will see you face to face? I am beginning to realize that your work of purification happens best in darkness, when you seem distant though you are near. Help me to have courage as I let go of what is false in order to reach into the darkness to take hold of what is true.

TURNING STONES
TO BREAD

⁓⧞⁓

After fasting forty days and forty nights, [Jesus] was hungry. The tempter came to him and said, "If you are the Son of God, tell these stones to become bread."

Matthew 4:2–3

After forty days in the wilderness, it would have been easy for Jesus to picture stones turning to bread. What starving man wouldn't? Like bread, the smooth, round stones fit snugly into the palm of his hand. He could almost smell the loaves baking in the desert heat. He had only to speak a word to perform this small miracle. But he didn't. Instead, he reminded the devil, "Man does not live on bread alone, but on every word that comes from the mouth of God."

Later, Jesus would tell the crowds, "I am the bread of life. He who comes to me shall never go hungry" (John 6:35). And again he spoke of bread: "Which of you, if his son asks for bread, will give him a stone?... If you ... know how to give good gifts to your children, how much more will your Father in heaven give good gifts to those who ask him" (Matthew 7:9–11).

Yet despite our faith, sometimes we are hungry. And sometimes we are tempted to believe that God has handed us a stone when we asked for bread. We plead for the bread of financial blessing, and we go bankrupt. We ask for the bread of a loving spouse, and we remain single. We beg for the bread of success, and we fail. Where is this bread that Jesus speaks of that we are so hungry for? If we had the power to turn our stones to bread, we would do so in an instant.

Yet sometimes we do have that power. We can cheat to obtain the money we want. We can sleep around to get the love we need. We can play games and dirty tricks to get ahead. And for a while, this bread will feed us. But it will never satisfy.

Jesus wasn't exaggerating when he called himself the bread of life. He's the one who nourishes our souls. If you have tried but failed to satisfy your cravings, bring them to Jesus once again. Spend some time quietly in his presence. Tell him what you are feeling and ask him to show you the truth of his Word and of his promise. It may be that your hunger will lead you to a deeper experience of his sufficiency.

Lord, you have created us with spiritual hungers, cravings that are not easily satisfied. Help me to resist the temptation to stuff myself with cheap substitutes, and, instead, help me to pursue you as the source of my life. When I am tempted to turn stones to bread through my own power, give me courage to trust your Word so that it will nourish my soul.

A Temporary Miracle

~≈~

The eternal God is your refuge, and underneath are the ever-lasting arms.

Deuteronomy 33:27

Dan and Dale Goorhouse were more than brothers. They were identical twins and best friends who roomed together in college. After they married, they lived just two blocks apart. As far as they knew, they would spend the rest of their lives working hard, raising their children, and one day recognizing their own age-worn features in each other's faces. But suddenly that familiar and comforting vision of the future vanished. Without warning, Dale was diagnosed with lung cancer.

"It was such a shock," Dan explained. "Dale was an athlete. Someone who ate right and who took care of himself. He never even smoked. We just couldn't believe he had lung cancer. He and I were products of the same environment. We shared the same genetic make-up. How could he possibly be sick when I was perfectly healthy? I couldn't stop asking the question.

"His doctors prescribed the most aggressive course of chemotherapy they could. After he completed it, they performed a CAT scan, which revealed spots on his liver, one kidney, and his spine. Dale's oncologist was almost certain the cancer had spread. If it had, surgery to remove the cancerous lung would be pointless. If not, it might save his other lung and his life.

"Neither Dale nor I were very religious at that time. We had been brought up in the Mormon church but had left it in our late teens. Since then, we had attended a couple of different Christian churches, but we weren't too serious about it. They say that in foxholes even atheists believe in God. I guess cancer was that foxhole for Dale and me. Both of us began to pray for a miracle along with our entire family. None of us were ready for Dale to die.

"It happened when Dale was alone, lying on a gurney, waiting to go in for another set of X-rays. He was praying that God would heal his kidney and liver, erasing the spots so that the doctors would have enough confidence to remove the cancerous lung. He asked God to give him a sign that he heard his prayers, and then something very strange happened. Dale told me that he felt his body being lifted off the gurney. For a few moments, he was simply suspended in the air.

"There was no rational explanation for what happened to him. Even so, he wasn't the least bit afraid. Instead, he said he felt an incredible sense of peace. He knew then that the doctors wouldn't find those spots. He was so sure, he even told the X-ray technician that nothing would show up on the film.

"And Dale was right. The oncologist was extremely surprised when he reviewed the X-rays and found no evidence of cancer. The whole family felt that God had done something wonderful for Dale. It was the beginning of real faith for us all.

"The doctors performed the surgery, and Dale just got stronger and stronger. For five months he felt great. His hair grew back, and he looked the picture of health. But then, almost two years after the initial diagnosis, the doctors found cancer in the other lung. Though I became physically ill when Dale told me the news, he assured me that he was at peace about it — and I knew he was. He encouraged me to stop worrying because everything was in God's hands.

"We learned of the cancer's recurrence in January. Dale died on February 25. Looking back on it, I'm not sure why God healed him only temporarily. But I do know that my family and I will never be the same because of what happened. It gave us time to deal with his death, and it made us closer as a family. Our faith is so much stronger now.

"Somehow, I drew strength from the way Dale handled himself. I am proud of how much courage and trust he showed. Now I try to teach my own boys to love and appreciate each other, realizing that life is such a fragile thing."

Dan and his family are grateful for the miracle that Dale experienced even if it simply delayed his death by a few months. Somehow, it must have convinced Dale that God was real and that he was in charge of everything that happened. Through the days that preceded his death, he may well have felt the strong arms of God still holding him, just like that day he was raised up on the gurney.

He may even have realized that every healing is really only temporary. Each of us will one day die. We will certainly lose the people we love the most. But such miracles help convince us that God is near, tenderly carrying us in his arms, watching over us as we let go of this life to take hold of the next.

Father, you are our refuge in time of trouble. No one can comfort us like you do. No one has arms powerful and tender enough to hold us when we are sick and hurting. Help us to remember that these are the very same arms that will one day raise us from our graves to enjoy everlasting life in your presence.

A BETTER WAY THAN MIRACLES

*An angel of the Lord appeared to Joseph in a dream. "Get up,"
he said, "take the child and his mother and escape to Egypt.
Stay there until I tell you, for Herod is going to search for
the child to kill him." ... When Herod realized he had been
outwitted by the Magi, he was furious, and he gave orders to
kill all the boys in Bethlehem and its vicinity who were two
years old and under.*

Matthew 2:13, 16

An angel warned Joseph to flee Bethlehem from the wrath of
a wicked king. And Joseph heeded the warning. Through a
miracle, God saved his infant son. Yet many baby boys were slaughtered in Jesus' stead. Why was there no miracle for them? Why does
there seem to be no miracle for so many innocent children today?

Recently, I watched a television documentary that broke my
heart. It was an exposé of the consequences of China's "one-child
policy." Because of overpopulation, the Chinese government has
made it unlawful for a family to have more than one child. Because
Chinese culture values males more than females, millions of baby
girls have been aborted or abandoned. Those that have been abandoned often die in orphanages, where conditions are unspeakable.

Such stories force us to confront the most difficult question in
the world. Why does God allow evil? Why does he perform miracles for a few of us, while the many suffer? Easy answers elude us.

In Herod's case, God chose not to contravene the will of a wicked ruler. In fact, this seems to be his preferred style of relating to human beings, both good and evil. He allows us the freedom of choice, though, eventually, we are judged as to how well or poorly we use that freedom. Inevitably, our misuse of it has the power to destroy others.

Sometimes, though, evil is rampant because good people stand by and do nothing. Unlike us, God realizes that supernatural acts of power are not always the most effective method for diminishing evil. Instead, he tells us to overcome evil with good. He prefers to unleash the power of his love through ordinary men and women, who decide to shelter the homeless, adopt a child, or find ways to bring solace to the afflicted.

Whatever God is asking, try to be generous. Who knows whether he may want to mold you into a living miracle, a flesh-and-blood answer to someone else's prayer?

Father, I pray that the grief I feel when confronted by tragedy will be harnessed for your purposes. Rather than feeling oppressed by evil, let me seek to be an instrument in your hand. Unite me with others, so that together our love might be a light that overcomes the darkness.

THE DANGERS
OF THE GOSPEL

~≋∽

On Herod's birthday the daughter of Herodias danced for them and pleased Herod so much that he promised with an oath to give her whatever she asked. Prompted by her mother, she said, "Give me here on a platter the head of John the Baptist."

Matthew 14:6–8

Jesus called his cousin John the greatest man who ever lived. Yet John languished in prison and was cruelly murdered in the midst of Herod's birthday celebration. His head on a platter must have made for a macabre ending to that particular party.

What had John done to deserve this fate? He had spoken the simple truth, declaring that Herod and Herodias were unlawfully married because she had already been wed to Philip, Herod's brother. By so doing, John made a deadly enemy.

After John's death, the disciples must have recalled Jesus' words: "Anyone who does not take his cross and follow me is not worthy of me. Whoever finds his life will lose it, and whoever loses his life for my sake will find it" (Matthew 10:38–39). John had not shirked his cross. He had spoken the truth and paid the ultimate price.

Were the disciples shocked by what happened to John? Did they have second thoughts about following Jesus? Certainly they must have realized the dangerous climate in which their Master moved. Perhaps for the first time, they realized that he really meant what he said: "Do not suppose that I have come to bring peace to the earth. I did not come to bring peace, but a sword" (Matthew 10:34). "All men will hate you because of me, but he who stands firm to the end will be saved" (10:22).

This is not the kind of message that most of us easily embrace. Instead we do our best to tame it by reducing the hard sayings of Jesus to the softness of metaphors. Rather than a tortured body hanging on a bloody cross, we see only the lovely gold crosses we wear around our necks. Or we limit the potency of his message by confining it to its historical context. Of course people suffered. But that was two thousand years ago, when Christianity was just getting started.

But the gospel is as dangerous today as it was when Jesus first preached it. It is an affront to evil that will be met with determined resistance, both within our hearts and in the world at large. Though we haven't the power to remove all the external barriers, we can ask God to demolish the obstacles within our souls. As we do, we will find that the presence of Jesus will grow strong within us, enabling us to do whatever he asks.

Lord, the effect of your Word is like a bucket of cold water thrown on a sleeping man. Wake me with the bracing freshness of the truth. Rather than bending your Word to make it fit me better, I ask that you would conform me to its power.

18

MIRACLES AND DREAMS

*How much there is in the Bible about dreams. There are,
I think, some sixteen chapters in the Old Testament and four
or five in the New in which dreams are mentioned, and there are
many other passages scattered throughout the book which refer
to visions. If we believe the Bible, we must accept the fact that,
in the old days, God and his angels came to men in their sleep
and made themselves known in dreams.*

Abraham Lincoln

More often than not, we ignore our dreams. The more colorful of these sometimes merit a morning's retelling, but after that we forget them. Bad dreams are chalked up to the exotic meal we consumed the night before or to a nagging anxiety that crept into our brain in the middle of the night. But that's about all the stock many of us place in our dreams.

But what if there's more to them than meets the eye? Can God ever speak to us through our dreams? A quick review of Scripture indicates that God spoke powerfully through dreams. A few of the biblical characters whose lives were affected by dreams included Abraham, Jacob, Joseph, Samuel, Saul, Solomon, Joseph (the father of Jesus), and the apostle Peter. In fact, the early Christian church believed that God sometimes revealed his will through dreams.

Though dreams are often complex and difficult to understand, I believe they may convey spiritual messages to those willing to listen. Of course there is danger in paying too much attention to our dreams. We can become overly introspective and unbalanced if we become obsessed with them, forgetting that dreams are just one avenue, and not the main one, by which God visits us.

In truth, our Creator can use whatever means he chooses to communicate with us. Perhaps he sometimes touches us while we sleep, because he knows we are more vulnerable then. A vivid dream may penetrate our defenses in a way that other methods of communication would not. At the very least, the stories that follow encourage us to be open to the variety of ways God works in our lives.

If you have been ignoring your dreams, it may be time to pay closer attention. As you do, remember to put your dreams into the context of what God has already revealed in his Word. And never make a big decision based only on a dream. Otherwise, you may mistake other voices for the voice of God.

A DREAM OF
AMAZING GRACE

*Then he showed me Joshua the high priest standing before
the angel of the LORD, and Satan standing at his right side to
accuse him. The LORD said to Satan, "The LORD rebuke you,
Satan! The LORD, who has chosen Jerusalem, rebuke you! Is
not this man a burning stick snatched from the fire?"*

Zechariah 3:1–2

John Newton is famous for having penned the well-known hymn
"Amazing Grace." Before his conversion, however, he lived anything but a Christian life as a seaman and slave trader. In his auto-
biography, he tells the story of a vivid dream he had, some twenty
years before he entered the ministry.

Newton dreamed he was standing on the deck of his ship one
night, in the harbor of Venice, when suddenly a man approached
and showed him a ring. The man gave the ring to the sailor, stress-
ing that it would bring him much happiness and success. He also
warned him that if he ever lost the ring, he would know only trouble and misery. Newton accepted the ring gladly, assuring the man
he would keep it safe.

As soon as the first man departed, a second man took his
place. He wasted no time but began to inquire about the ring.
Newton repeated what he had been told about its value, but this
man seemed surprised that anyone would ever be foolish enough to

place such importance on a mere ring. Before long, he was urging the sailor to toss it overboard. In the dream, Newton did just that, saying: "At last I plucked it off my finger and dropped it over the ship's side into the water; which it had no sooner touched, than I saw, the same instant, a terrible fire burst out from a range of the mountains [a part of the Alps], which appeared at some distance behind the city of Venice. I saw the hills ... and they were all in flames. I perceived, too late, my folly; and my tempter with an air of insult, informed me, that all the mercy God had in reserve for me was comprised in that ring which I had willfully thrown away. I understood that I must now go with him to the burning mountains.... I trembled, and was in a great agony."

The dream continued and Newton met another man, who asked him why he was so sad. He explained that he had ruined himself and deserved no pity. Then the man asked him whether he would be wiser the second time around if the ring were returned to him. Before Newton could respond, the stranger threw himself over the side of the boat and plunged beneath the surface of the water where the ring had been dropped. Then he surfaced with the ring in hand and climbed back aboard the ship. Immediately, the flames of the mountains were extinguished.

The dream troubled Newton for two or three days, so much so that he could hardly eat or sleep. But eventually he forgot about it. He would not think of it again for several years, when as he says, "I found myself in circumstances very nearly resembling those suggested by this extraordinary dream, when I stood helpless and hopeless upon the brink of an awful eternity."

Fortunately, John Newton became one of history's great converts and went on to write hymns that have inspired believers throughout the world. Like a brand plucked from the fire, he was eventually saved by the mercy of a loving God.

Amazing grace, how sweet the sound, that saved a wretch like me! I once was lost, but now am found, was blind but now I see. Through many dangers, toils, and snares, I have already come; 'tis grace has brought me safe thus far, and grace will lead me home.

SOMEONE WAS PRAYING

❧

When you walk through the fire, you will not be burned; the
flames will not set you ablaze.

Isaiah 43:2

Paul Grams had worked for many years as a firefighter for the city of Rockford, Illinois. Because of a remarkable experience he had several years ago, he knows that the veil between the natural and supernatural is not always as thick as we think.

"Firefighting is a dangerous profession, but that's what I signed up for. Unfortunately, it's harder to be married to a fireman than to be one; at least that's what my wife, Val, says. In fact, she usually has difficulty sleeping whenever I'm on duty. Strangely enough she slept peacefully through the early morning hours of April 3, 1995, when I was fighting for my life.

"Ron Hill, John Brazones, and I were veteran firefighters, so I wasn't worried when we were called to the scene of an apartment fire. A neighbor told us he thought an old woman and her grandchild might be trapped in the second-floor apartment. We had no way of knowing that neither of them was at home that night.

"The apartment was filled with dense smoke, so thick you couldn't see the beam from your own flashlight unless you held it right in front of your face. As soon as we realized we were alone in the apartment, we knew it was time to get out. Our tanks held 2,200 pounds of air pressure and we figured the warning bell might go off any minute, signaling that only five hundred pounds remained. Depending on conditions, that meant we would have just three to five minutes left to breathe. But the smoke was so dense we became disoriented. Remarkably, none of us panicked.

"By now we were crawling on the floor, feeling for a way out. A picture flashed through my mind of a photograph I had seen in a firefighter magazine. It showed hand prints in the soot on the wall where a firefighter had vainly searched for a window just a few inches away. He never made it out. Now I wondered if the three of us were about to become the next headline.

"Just then I bumped into someone. It happened several times. Each time I asked, 'John, is that you?' 'Ron, is that you?' No one answered, but I heard a voice in my head saying, 'You will never get out of here alive.' Despite our danger and the death sentence I had just heard, I felt complete peace. It was as though another voice, one I trusted, was also speaking to me: 'Don't worry, people are praying for you. You're going to be all right.' I assumed Val was praying, because she often awoke in the middle of the night to pray.

"Just then, John's bell went off. We kept groping but couldn't find a window. About three minutes passed and I knew John would soon be in trouble. Actually he had already run out of air and was holding his breath, desperate for a miracle, when his fingers found the glass. He smashed the window with both hands, and we all made it to safety. I was descending the rescue ladder just as the air in my own tank ran out. Due to a malfunction, my warning bell had never sounded.

"It was about 1:20 a.m. when we escaped the apartment, but our job wasn't done. The fire had begun in the basement, so we waded around in knee-deep water beneath the building to check for problems. We succeeded in safely extinguishing the fire by about 5 a.m.

"That day, my wife left for her job at a local elementary school. Later, she overheard a conversation that startled her. One of her coworkers, Sherry Zahorik, was telling a friend about the strange night she had just experienced. Sherry knew nothing about my being in a fire, so Val nearly fell off her chair when she heard the details of Sherry's dream. Here's what Sherry told her:

" 'I awoke at about 1:00 a.m. with such a heaviness on my chest I could hardly breathe. I felt I was supposed to pray for someone in trouble. As I was praying, a dream unfolded before my eyes. I could see three people in a completely dark room, covered by a very foggy-like smoke. I didn't know who they were, but I could see them frantically searching for something. I felt I was right there with them, watching them go through the whole thing. There was confusion and something worse than confusion—an evil presence that permeated the room. One of them kept bumping into something and calling the names of his friends, thinking it was them. Then this presence would laugh and say, "You will never get out of here alive." As I heard that voice, I saw a picture of a man clawing at a wall, trying to reach a window. The wall was full of nail scratching, and blood was running down the window.

" 'By this time I was out of bed, praying up a storm. Each time I would try to go back to sleep, the heaviness would return so strongly I couldn't breathe. I knew I had to keep praying until whatever it was was over. Finally, about 4:00 or 5:00 a.m., the pressure in my chest lifted and I felt at peace. It seemed to me the crisis had passed. Everything was going to be all right.'

"Anyone who has never been in a fire couldn't possibly have described it as accurately as Sherry did. The smoke can be so dense and dark that it blots out light and even deadens sound. Val knew enough about my experience to be absolutely bowled over by the story of Sherry's dream. Someone had been praying for me after all, countering a terrible presence in the darkness that was trying to destroy my hope.

"I know Sherry was given a vision that night to enable her to pray for us in the midst of a very desperate situation. Thanks to her prayers none of us panicked, depleting our air supply before we could escape the fire. By the grace of God, I am alive to tell the story."

Father, your ways are mysterious and wonderful. Thank you for your faithful, life-giving help.

THIS DREAM CAME TRUE

The LORD will watch over your coming and going both now and forevermore.

Psalm 121:7

J ody Lorenzen was in high school when she had a dream that may have saved three lives.

"My brother, Jonathan, and I were in Monterey, California. We had brought two friends with us for a two-week visit to my grandparents' home. My grandparents were generous with their car, and we had driven it around most of the time we were there. But it bothered me that I was the only one who wore a seat belt. I mentioned it a few times, but nobody paid any attention.

"After about a week and a half, I had a dream that we got in a terrible wreck. I don't remember the details, but I do remember the ambulance and the lights and the awful knowledge that I was the only one who survived. It was so horrible. I had to go home by myself and break the news to my family.

"I was never so glad to wake up from a dream.

"That day we decided to visit an amusement park about an hour away. As we drove, I told everyone about it, but just as before, they seemed to blow it off. On the way back, the two guys started goofing off in the front seat. Suddenly the car swerved and hit the median. We flipped and did a complete rollover. I was stunned but alive. It seemed as though my nightmare had come true. But when I opened my eyes, I realized everyone was fine. The top of the car looked like a pop can that somebody had stepped on. All the windows had shattered. Remarkably, all four of us had been wearing our seat belts. Each one of us walked away from the accident, grateful to be alive.

"One of the guys said, 'Jody, didn't you just have a dream about us getting in a wreck?' We all started talking at once, amazed that each of us had put our seat belts on when we got back into the car that day.

"You might think my dream was a product of anxiety, and maybe I was a bit anxious. But it's hard for me to believe that somebody upstairs didn't have an awful lot to do with it."

Father, thank you for watching over us in so many unexpected ways. Open our ears so that we can hear your voice more clearly in whatever form it comes.

THE WEDDING MIRACLE

When the wine was gone, Jesus' mother said to him, "They have no more wine." "Dear woman, why do you involve me?" Jesus replied. "My time has not yet come." His mother said to the servants, "Do whatever he tells you."

John 2:3–5

If anyone ever had perfect timing it was Jesus. He never missed a beat. In tune with his Father's will, he would only embark on his public ministry when God gave the go-ahead, not before. So why does he seem to change his mind so quickly? Why does he perform a miracle that started tongues wagging all over Galilee?

Somehow Jesus must have known that Mary's prayer had changed things, suddenly setting his public ministry in motion. His hidden life had come to an end. Now the light of the world would reveal itself, a counterpoint against the darkness.

Jesus wastes no time, ordering the servants at the wedding feast described in John's gospel to take six stone water jars, the kind the Jews used for ceremonial cleansing, and fill them with water. Then he tells them to call the steward so that he can draw out its contents and taste it. As soon as it passes his lips, the man recognizes it as the most exquisite wine he has ever tasted, and he cannot imagine why the bride and groom have withheld the best wine until last.

As usual, the miracle is about more than a simple wedding feast in Cana. It is about transforming the ordinary into the extraordinary, the natural into the supernatural, the kingdom of this world

188

telling a friend his dream.
round loaf of barley bread
e camp. It struck the tent
urned and collapsed." His
thing other than the sword
e. God has given the Midi-
s hands."

Judges 7:13–14

childhood. One day, as I was
led to our home, I was startled
thing out of a Saturday morn-
ring across a lawn, one in hot
lassic case of dog chasing cat,
tiny chipmunk was furiously
dog. I'm not certain whether
deranged.

lianites remind me of that fero-
. Gideon was the leader of the
efore attacking the Midianite
ps. He didn't want Gideon and
he coming victory. It wasn't just
arm behind his back. Before he
31,700 men from a total force of

32,000. He was left with less than one percent of his army to fight an enemy that was too numerous to count.

Still, God assured him of victory and invited Gideon to eavesdrop on the enemy before attacking. That's when Gideon overheard the man's dream. As soon as he heard it, he worshiped God and returned to his camp to rally the troops. Together, three hundred men found a way to trick the Midianites into thinking they were an enormous army. As soon as the Israelites blew their trumpets, their enemies awoke to pandemonium. Filled with terror and divinely inspired confusion, they turned on each other with their swords and then fled.

That day God did what only God can do: he used the weak and powerless to rout the strong and mighty. He used three hundred men to defeat an army of many thousands.

I must admit that the tactics of God sometimes make me extremely uncomfortable. In fact, he often asks us to do things in a way that contradicts our most basic instincts. Jesus himself excelled at this: "If someone strikes you on the right cheek, turn to him the other also" (Matthew 5:39). "If someone forces you to go one mile, go with him two miles" (5:41). "Love your enemies and pray for those who persecute you" (5:44).

God's ways scandalize us because they contradict the basic values of our fallen world, the only world we have ever really known. Without the gifts of grace and faith, we could not possibly respond as he desires. But with them, we can learn to trust in a God who never fails and never forsakes us, a God whose word is true and whose wisdom is deeper than anything we can comprehend.

Father, you know that Gideon didn't start out as a man of faith, but that he became one because of your faithfulness. Help me to remember how faithful you have been in my own life so that I may be quick to trust you, quick to say yes, despite my fears.

"I Dreamed of
a Golden City"

⤞⤙

*Your old men will dream dreams, your young men will see
visions.*

Joel 2:28

Rarely are we in a position to interpret the dreams of others. Most often, the dreamer needs to validate the meaning of the dream in his or her own life. But sometimes the dreamer may need help interpreting a significant dream. A graduate of Yale University, Paul Thigpen is the author of many books and has served as assistant professor of religious studies at Southwest Missouri State University. On tour in Europe during the 1970s with the Yale University Glee Club, Paul heard the story of a piercingly beautiful dream, confided to him by a fellow student. He has never forgotten it.

"Mark and I had become good friends during our summer tour of Europe. He was a nice Jewish kid from New York who knew so little about his religious heritage that he wouldn't have recognized Moses if he spotted him strolling through the Red Sea. While he knew next-to-nothing about the Old Testament, his knowledge of Jesus and the New Testament was simply nonexistent.

"One day, Mark had a severe allergic reaction to something in the air — for him a frequent problem. Though he carried medicine with him in the event of an attack, he usually had to get emergency medical treatment if he didn't take the medicine quickly enough. This time, as he began to choke up and worried aloud that he might need a doctor, I offered to pray for him and he said yes. Remarkably, the reaction subsided. That experience must have impressed him, because one morning he came to me and said, 'Paul, I've had a dream and I believe you're the one who's supposed to interpret it.' I was studying religion at Yale, not dream interpretation, but I told him I'd be glad to listen.

" 'In my dream,' he explained, 'I was standing with a friend looking up into the sky and in the sky was a beautiful golden city. As soon as we saw it, we knew we wanted to get there. But we didn't know how. Suddenly, we saw a tree that seemed to be engulfed in flames. It kept burning but it wasn't consumed. We got the idea that if we could climb that tree, we could reach the golden city. But whenever we tried, we were forced to give up because the fire was so intense. We fell back and began to cry and tell each other we would never get there.

" 'But then I heard a voice that seemed to come from above us. It was the sound of a man groaning in pain, and I knew he was dying, and the strangest thing is that I also knew he was God. But how could someone be both man and God, and if he was God how could he be dying, I kept asking myself. When the groaning stopped, I knew the man was dead, and suddenly I thought that maybe we could make it to that golden city after all. But as we approached the tree, I heard another voice saying, "Not until the morning of the third day." '

" 'Paul, none of this makes any sense to me. Do you know what it means?'

"I was so astonished by the dream that I blurted out: 'Well, you're Jewish, aren't you? Don't you know the story of Moses and the burning bush?' He didn't.

" 'The Old Testament,' I explained, 'tells how God appeared to Moses in a bush that burned without burning up. The burning bush represents the presence of God. And Scripture talks about the golden city being the kingdom of heaven waiting for us. But we can't make it there on our own efforts because we lack holiness. In your dream, the fire in the tree represents the holiness of God. Without being purified, the fire would destroy us before we reached heaven.'

" 'But what about the man who was also God?' he asked.

" 'Don't you know that Christians believe Jesus was both man and God and that he was crucified?'

"He didn't.

" 'Christians believe,' I continued, 'that Jesus had to die on a cross—a tree—before the way would be open for us to heaven. Furthermore, the gospel story tells us that Jesus was lifeless until the morning of the third day, when he rose from the dead and later ascended to the Father, opening the gate of heaven for us.'

"Mark looked at me wide-eyed all the time I was speaking. Despite asking me to interpret his dream, he was astonished it made sense to me. After that we lost touch, and I don't know what became of him. But I do know one thing: that dream came from a source totally beyond Mark. While he was sleeping, God lifted the curtain between heaven and earth so that Mark would one day have a chance to reach the city in his dream."

Lord, thank you for pursuing us when we were yet so far from you. I pray that you will open the eyes of the blind and the ears of the deaf. Give them an open heart to receive the gospel.

BIBLIOGRAPHY

Adler, Mortimer. *The Angels and Us*. New York: Macmillan, 1982.

Anderson, Joan Wester. *Where Angels Walk*. New York: Ballantine, 1992.

Brown, Colin. *Miracles and the Critical Mind*. Grand Rapids: Eerdmans, 1984.

Buttrick, George A., ed. *The Interpreter's Dictionary of the Bible*. Nashville: Abingdon, 1962.

Freedman, David Noel, ed. *Anchor Bible Dictionary*. 6 volumes. New York: Doubleday, 1992.

Graham, Billy. *Angels: God's Secret Agents*. Waco: Word, 1986.

Henry, Matthew. *Matthew Henry's Commentary on the Whole Bible*. Various publishers.

Herring, Wayne C. "Angelology," unpublished sermon.

Kinnaman, Gary. *Angels Dark and Light*. Ann Arbor, MI: Servant, 1994.

Lockyer, Herbert. *All the Miracles of the Bible*. Grand Rapids: Zondervan, 1961.

MacGregor, Geddes. *Angels*. New York: Paragon, 1988.

Marshall, Catherine. *Meeting God at Every Turn*. Grand Rapids: Chosen, 1980.

McInerny, Ralph. *Miracles: A Catholic View*. Huntington, IN: Our Sunday Visitor, 1986.

McKenzie, John L. *Dictionary of the Bible*. New York: Macmillan, 1965.

Monden, Louis. *Signs and Wonders*. New York: Desclee, 1966.

O'Sullivan, Paul. *All about Angels*. Rockford, IL: Tan, 1945.

Ronner, John. *Do You Have a Guardian Angel?* Murfreesboro, TN: Mamre, 1985.

———. *Know Your Angels*. Murfreesboro, TN: Mamre, 1993.

Unger, Merrill F. *Unger's Bible Dictionary*. Chicago: Moody Press, 1957, 1961, 1966.

Valentine, Mary Hester. *Miracles*. Chicago: Thomas More, 1988.

Wakefield, Dan. *Expect a Miracle*. San Francisco: HarperSanFrancisco, 1995.

Sitting at the Feet of Rabbi Jesus

How the Jewishness of Jesus Can Transform Your Faith

Ann Spangler and Lois Tverberg

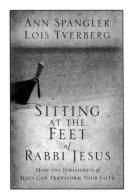

A rare chance to know Jesus as his first disciples knew him.

What would it be like to journey back to the first century and sit at the feet of Rabbi Jesus as one of his Jewish disciples? How would your understanding of the gospel have been shaped by the customs, beliefs, and traditions of the Jewish culture in which you lived?

Sitting at the Feet of Rabbi Jesus takes you on a fascinating tour of the Jewish world of Jesus, offering inspirational insights that can transform your faith. Ann Spangler and Lois Tverberg paint powerful scenes from Jesus' ministry, immersing you in the prayers, feasts, history, culture, and customs that shaped Jesus and those who followed him.

You will hear the parables as they must have sounded to first-century Jews, powerful and surprising. You will join the conversations that were already going on among the rabbis of his day. You will watch with new understanding as the events of his life unfold. And you will emerge with new excitement about the roots of your own Christian faith.

Sitting at the Feet of Rabbi Jesus will change the way you read Scripture and deepen your understanding of the life of Jesus. It will also help you to adapt the rich prayers and customs you learn about to your own life, in ways that both respect and enrich your Christian faith.

Hardcover, Jacketed: 978-0-310-28422-2

The Tender Words of God

A Daily Guide

Ann Spangler

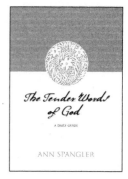

Over the years, Ann Spangler has read through the Bible several times from Genesis to Revelation. But like many people who tend to be self-critical, Ann found it easier to absorb the harsher-sounding passages in the Bible than those that speak of God's love and compassion.

Then one day, Ann listened as her friend Joan talked about a time in her life when she became convinced of God's love. Ann expected her friend to reveal something complicated and difficult, a tragedy, perhaps, that God had brought her through. But Joan had simply decided to set aside one month in which she would act as though God loved her. And that settled it for her—for good.

In the months that followed, Ann decided to develop a remedial course in which she could reflect morning and evening on the most tender words of God in the Bible. She prayed that God's penetrating Word would transform her as she hunted through Scripture for words of mercy, compassion, peace, and protection.

The *Tender Words of God* is the result of this process, offering ninety days of devotional readings on some of Scripture's most encouraging words. While the core of the book is Scripture, each week contains reflections and daily prayers that chronicle Ann's struggle to know God better. Ann invites you to join her on this journey to know God better, to let his tender words become like guardians at the beginning and at the end of each day, convincing you once and for all of his faithful, committed love.

Hardcover, Jacketed: 978-0-310-26716-4

Women of the Bible

A One-Year Devotional Study of Women in Scripture

Ann Spangler and Jean E. Syswerda

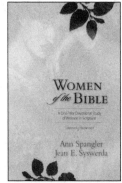

Women of the Bible focuses on fifty-two remarkable women in Scripture — women whose struggles to live with faith and courage are not unlike your own. And now this bestselling devotional study book has been updated and expanded to enhance its flexibility, usefulness, and relevance for both individuals and groups.

Small groups will especially welcome the way the Bible studies have been streamlined to fit the unique needs of the group setting.

Vital and deeply human, the women in this book encourage you through their failures as well as their successes. You'll see how God acted in surprising and wonderful ways to draw them — and you — to himself. This year-long devotional offers a unique method to help you slow down and savor the story of God's unrelenting love for his people, offering a fresh perspective that will nourish and strengthen your personal communion with him.

Hardcover, Jacketed: 978-0-310-27055-3

Pick up a copy today at your favorite bookstore!

Men of the Bible

A One-Year Devotional Study of Men in Scripture

Ann Spangler and Robert Wolgemuth

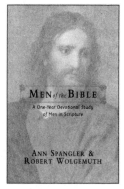

Men of the Bible takes a close-up look at fifty-two men in Scripture — complex flesh-and-blood characters whose strengths and weaknesses often seem strangely similar to our own. Heroes and villains, sinners and prophets, commoners and kings … their dramatic life stories provide us with fresh perspective on the unfolding story of redemption.

Though our culture differs vastly from theirs, the fundamental issues we face in relation to God and the world remain the same. We still reach for great dreams and selfish ambitions. We wrestle with fear and indecision, struggle with sexual temptation, and experience the ache of loneliness and the devastation of betrayal. And, like many of these men, we long to walk more closely with the God who calls us into an intimate relationship with himself and who enables us to fulfill his purpose for our lives.

Designed for personal prayer and study or for use in small groups, *Men of the Bible* will help you make Bible reading a daily habit. Whether you dip into portions or read every page, this book will help you grow in character, wisdom, and obedience as a person after God's own heart.

Hardcover, Jacketed: 978-0-310-23944-4

Pick up a copy today at your favorite bookstore!

ZONDERVAN®
.com

Praying the Names of God

A Daily Guide

Ann Spangler

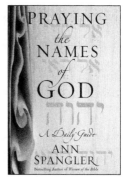

Names in the ancient world did more than simply distinguish one person from another; they often conveyed the essential nature and character of a person. This is especially true when it comes to the names of God recorded in the Bible. *Praying the Names of God* explores the primary names and titles of God in the Old Testament to reveal the deeper meanings behind them.

El Shadday, Elohim, Adonay, Abba, El Elyon — God Almighty, Mighty Creator, Lord, Father, God Most High — these are just a few of the names and titles of God that yield rich insights into his nature and character. *Praying the Names of God* shows readers how to study and pray God's names by focusing each week on one of the primary names or titles of God.

- Monday — readers study a portion of Scripture that reveals the name.
- Tuesday–Thursday — readers pray specific Scripture passages related to the name.
- Friday — readers pray Scripture promises connected to the name.

By incorporating the divine names and titles into their prayers — and learning about the biblical context in which the name was revealed — readers will gain a more intimate understanding of who God is and how he can be relied on in every circumstance of their lives.

Hardcover, Jacketed: 978-0-310-25353-2

Praying the Names of Jesus

A Daily Guide

Ann Spangler

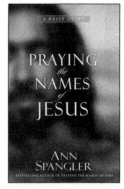

Joy, peace, and power — these are only some of the gifts promised to those who trust in the name of the Lord. *Praying the Names of Jesus* will lead readers into a richer and more rewarding relationship with Christ by helping them to understand and to pray his names on a daily basis. By understanding the biblical context in which these names and titles were revealed, readers will gain a more intimate knowledge of Jesus and of his plan for their lives. They will also begin to see how each of his names holds within it a promise: to be our Teacher, Healer, Friend, and Lord — to be God with Us no matter the circumstances.

Prince of Peace, Lamb of God, Bread of Life, Yeshua ... through his names and titles, we come to understand more fully how Jesus reveals God's heart to us. *Praying the Names of Jesus* focuses on twenty-six of his most prominent names and titles to provide six months' worth of devotions. Each week provides a unique devotional program designed for personal prayer and study or for use in small groups. *Praying the Names of Jesus* is the companion volume to the bestselling *Praying the Names of God*. In ways both surprising and profound it reveals a rich portrait of Jesus that will move readers toward a deeper experience of his love and mercy.

Hardcover, Jacketed: 978-0-310-25345-7